FENG SHUI
WITH ARCHANGELS,
UNICORNS, AND DRAGONS

"Franziska shows you how to welcome into your life archangels, unicorns, and dragons with their amazing love and wisdom. I loved the visualizations and meditations and found the exercises powerful and practical. Timeless wisdom is woven into every page. This exceptional book, a significant addition to the genre, will raise your consciousness and change the way you live your life. Franziska is a master of combining ancient wisdom and esoteric knowledge—her best book yet."

—CAMILLA JOHNSON SMITH, group psychotherapist, counsellor, healer, and teacher with the Diana Cooper School of White Light

"When I moved with my family to our new home, the first thing I did was light a candle and connect to the angel of our home. I have had a deep connection with this beautiful angel since, so I was very surprised when she was so thrilled for me to do the course 'Feng Shui with Archangels, Unicorns, and Dragons.' And what an amazing journey we all had—the house angel, me, and all other light beings working for beautiful, high energy in my house! My home became a living place, truly filled with Love and Light! Filled with beautiful, pure energies, I now connect to my soul and work intentionally with angels, dragons, and unicorns to bring in abundance, fulfilment, joy, and good health. Franziska will show you how to manifest the highest good for yourself and your beloved family with help from angels, dragons, and unicorns, and this book will change your life forever! I recommend it from my heart to all of you beautiful souls who would like to bring true abundance, fulfilment, and harmony into your life and those closest to you!"

—MELINDA MARTON, spiritual teacher and author of
Sacred Connection with Trees

FENG SHUI

WITH ARCHANGELS, UNICORNS, AND DRAGONS

How to Transform the Energies of Your Home and Life

FRANZISKA SIRAGUSA

FINDHORN PRESS

Findhorn Press
One Park Street
Rochester, Vermont 05767
www.findhornpress.com

Findhorn Press is a division of Inner Traditions International

Disclaimer
The information in this book is given in good faith and intended for information
only. Neither author nor publisher can be held liable by any person for any loss or
damage whatsoever which may arise directly or indirectly from the use of this book
or any of the information therein.

Cataloging-in-Publication data for this title is available from the Library of Congress

ISBN 979-8-88850-225-9 (print)
ISBN 979-8-88850-226-6 (ebook)

Printed and bound in the United States by Lake Book Manufacturing, LLC

10 9 8 7 6 5 4 3 2 1

Edited by Nicky Leach
Illustration by Tanielle Pink
Text design and layout by Damian Keenan
This book was typeset in Adobe Garamond Pro and Barlow Condensed with
Raleway used as a display typeface.

To send correspondence to the author of this book, mail a first-class letter to the
author c/o Inner Traditions • Bear & Company, One Park Street, Rochester,
VT 05767, USA and we will forward the communication, or contact the author
directly at **https://franziskasiragusa.com**.

With much gratitude,

I dedicate this book

to my dragon, Wei,

to honour our deep

and loving connection.

CONTENTS

Foreword *by Diana Cooper* 13
Preface 15

INTRODUCTION – Higher Help from the Angelic Realms 17
Introducing Angels 18
Introducing Unicorns 23
Introducing Dragons 24

10 WEEKS TO TRANSFORM YOUR LIFE AND HOME

PREPARATION WEEK
Seven Steps to Prepare for the Journey through the Bagua

STEP 1 – The Angel of Your Home 29
STEP 2 – Activate Your Crystals to Work with You 31
STEP 3 – Clear the Space below Your Home with an Earth Dragon 34
STEP 4 – Clear the Space that Contains Your Home
with Dragons and Angels 35
STEP 5 – Declutter with Your Home Transformation Team 37
STEP 6 – The 5D Bagua of Higher Aspirations 39
5D Bagua of Higher Aspirations 41
STEP 7 – The Entrance to Your Home 42

WEEK 1
KAN – Your Life Mission

BAGUA AREA 1 – KAN – Your Life Mission 45
Water Dragon Note 46
VISUALIZATION to Clear the Kan Area with a Water Dragon 47

Unicorns 48

VISUALIZATION to Meet Your Personal Unicorn and Receive Its Name .. 52

Meet Archangel Gabriel 52

VISUALIZATION to Activate Your Life Mission with
the Diamond Unicorns 53

The Power of Numbers and the Cosmic Turtle 56

CONNECT with the Number One 57

Intention for the Kan Area of Your Life 57

WEEK 2
KUN – Your Beautiful Open Heart

BAGUA AREA 2 – KUN – Your Beautiful Open Heart 58

Meet Archangel Chamuel 60

VISUALIZATION to Clear the Kun Area 61

Personal Dragon Note 61

VISUALIZATION to Meet Your Personal Dragon and Receive Its Name 64

Meet the Goddess Kuan Yin 65

VISUALIZATION with Kuan Yin to Open Your Heart to Divine Feminine
Love and Forgiveness 66

CONNECT with the Number Two 69

Intention for the Kun Area of Your Life 70

WEEK 3
ZHEN – The Gifts of the Ancestors

BAGUA AREA 3 – ZHEN – The Gifts of the Ancestors 71

VISUALIZATION to Clear the Zhen Area 72

Your Immediate Ancestors 73

Karma Note 73

The 12 Lords of Karma 73

VISUALIZATION to Honour Your Immediate Ancestors 75

Your Parents 77

VISUALIZATION to Meet Your Parents in Their Spirit Body 78

Cosmic Parents for the New Golden Age 80

VISUALIZATION to Meet Your Cosmic Parents 80

CONNECT with the Number Three 83

Intention for the Zhen Area of Your Life 83

WEEK 4
XUN – Open Up to Abundance

BAGUA AREA 4 – XUN – Open Up to Abundance 84

Air Dragon Note 85

Meet Archangel Raphael 86

VISUALIZATION to Clear the Xun Area 87

Reflections on My Xun Area 88

Activating Your Abundance Codes 89

The 12-Chakra System, according to Diana Cooper 89

VISUALIZATION to Activate Your Abundance Codes 93

CONNECT with the Number Four 95

Intention for the Xun Area of Your Life 96

WEEK 5
TAIJI Centre – Balance and Glorious Health

BAGUA AREA 5 – TAIJI Centre – Balance and Glorious Health 97

Meet Ascended Master Serapis Bey 98

VISUALIZATION to Clear the Taiji Centre and Activate It with
a Crystal or an Ascension Column 99

Meet Archangel Jophiel 101

Meet Archangel Mary 102

Meet Archangel Sandalphon 103

Meet Archangel Zadkiel 104

Cosmic Diamond Violet Flame Note 105

VISUALIZATION to Activate Your Taiji Centre with a Portal of Light 105

Your Health 106

11D Energy of Regeneration from Helios Note 107

Yin and Yang Dragons Note 108

VISUALIZATION to Restore Balance and Glorious Health 109

CONNECT with the Number Five 112

   Intention for the Taiji Area of Your Life 113

WEEK 6
QIAN – Incredible Higher Support

BAGUA AREA 6 – QIAN – Incredible Higher Support 114

VISUALIZATION to Clear the Qian Area 115

Guardian Angel Note 116

VISUALIZATION to Receive Your Guardian Angel's Name 118

Archangels 120

Meet Archangel Uriel 120

VISUALIZATION to Visit Your Overlighting Archangel 121

CONNECT with the Number Six 124

   Intention for the Qian Area of Your Life 124

WEEK 7
DUI – Never-Ending Creativity

BAGUA AREA 7 – DUI – Never-Ending Creativity 125

VISUALIZATION to Clear the Dui Area 126

Be Creative 127

VISUALIZATION to Bring Forth Your Creativity 127

CONNECT with the Number Seven 129

   Intention for the Dui Area of Your Life 129

WEEK 8
GEN – Embodying Your Soul and Accessing Its Wisdom

BAGUA AREA 8 – GEN – Embodying Your Soul and
Accessing Its Wisdom 130

VISUALIZATION to Clear the Gen Area 131

Your Evolution and the Soul Merge 132

Meet Archangel Mariel 133

Meet Ascended Master Lord Kuthumi 134

VISUALIZATION to Accelerate Your Evolution and Embody Your Soul 135
CONNECT with the Number Eight 138
    Intention for the Gen Area of Your Life 139

WEEK 9
LI – Your True Magnificence

BAGUA AREA 9 – LI – Your True Magnificence 140
Monad Note 140
Personal Note on My Li Area 141
VISUALIZATION to Clear the Li Area 141
EXERCISE: Who Are You? 142
Your Evolution and the Monadic Merge 142
Meet Archangel Metatron 143
VISUALIZATION to Merge with Your Monad 144
CONNECT with the Number Nine 147
    Intention for the Li Area of Your Life 147

Summary 148

CONCLUSION – Serious Decluttering 151

Bibliography 153
Exercises and Visualizations 154
About the Author 157
Index 158

Foreword

I have known Franziska for many years. She is a principal teacher of the Diana Cooper School and has applied herself wholeheartedly to her spiritual life. I did not know she had accomplished so much.

Now, she has written this fascinating book about feng shui. Indeed, her book offers much more than information about feng shui, for it introduces angels, unicorns, and dragons.

She explains how, working with the principles of energy flow, these glorious high-frequency beings have a tremendous impact on how your home feels and what happens there. The answers to what your dragon, angel, and unicorn can do for you are simply and clearly spelt out, with tips on how to interact with them. She includes beautiful information about different crystals and how to use them to enhance the effects of feng shui.

Most of all, this book is positive, inspirational, and full of light.

I love all the stories and personal examples that Franziska shares as she explores and learns for herself, so that I feel I know her and her home. They make the science of feng shui come to life, and I can't wait to apply the principles to my own home.

It is a book to keep by your bedside to refer to constantly as you transform your life.

Diana Cooper

Preface

The 10-week programme outlined in this book contains guidance and visualizations to transform your home and your life. Working through the 10 chapters will take you on a journey of discovery, unlock gifts, and activate the flow of cosmic abundance. The programme will help you become soul-conscious and acknowledge your magnificent divine self. It will help you heal your relationships, align you with your life purpose, and improve your health.

I'd never thought I would write a book with the word "feng shui" in the title. This ancient Chinese practice has always attracted me, and I have applied its principles to my previous homes but not yet to my current apartment. When I moved here three years ago, I used my intuition to place furniture and belongings. So when one day my guides dropped the title "Feng Shui with Archangels, Unicorns, and Dragons" into my mind, I was quite surprised, but at the same time, it resonated, and the structure of the book started to take shape.

Angels, unicorns, and dragons are part of my daily life. My mission is to connect people with these high-frequency beings from the angelic realms, and I train people to become certified angel, unicorn, or dragon teachers. I thought that combining the powerful energies of these higher beings with feng shui was a wonderful idea.

In Chinese, feng shui (*fēngshuǐ* 風水) literally means "wind-water." From ancient times, these forces were thought to direct the flow of the universal energies, or *qì*, which must be unimpeded for perfect health. Feng shui is a traditional Chinese practice that uses energy to harmonize people with their surroundings.

Feng shui is based on the belief that the arrangements of objects, structures, and space can affect the flow of energy and influence different aspects of your life, such as your relationships, career, and prosperity. By tidying, organizing, and positioning elements within a space in a way that promotes the smooth flow of energy, feng shui aims to create peace, balance, and harmony in your home and life. It encourages a positive and supportive atmosphere, leading to wellbeing, success, and living your life fully. By positively manipulating energy, feng shui can improve a situation and raise the frequency of vibration in a space.

Who better than these celestial beings to help with that? This book aims to help you raise the frequency of all areas in your home to the frequency of love and the frequency of your soul and Monad. Remember that your own energy, your personal *qi*, is also very powerful because you are a part of Source and representing the Divine Spirit in your own unique way.

We will work with the angel of your home, your guardian angel, the mighty archangels, and the unicorns and dragons. The goddess Kuan Yin and the ascended masters Serapis Bey and Lord Kuthumi have also stepped forward to help, and you will connect with your personal unicorn and your personal dragon. Enjoy this journey to a more beautiful home and onto a higher path!

Higher Help from the Angelic Realms

Angels, unicorns, and dragons belong to the angelic realms. Who better than them to transform your home into a sacred high-frequency space? Reading about angels raises your frequency, and when you connect and attune to them, they bring magic into your home and miracles into your life.

Right now, Source is directing millions of angels, unicorns, and dragons to Earth to assist with the dimensional shift that Earth is undergoing and help humanity prepare for a new Golden Age. The key to connecting with them is an open heart and raising your frequency.

What is the new Golden Age?

Humans have not always been three-dimensional and self-centred in the ways we have witnessed in the last 10,000 years. There have been various Golden Ages on Earth; for example, the Golden Age of Atlantis or the Golden Age of Lemuria, when the frequency of the people was fifth-dimensional. After the vibrations dropped, many higher beings withdrew from our planet.

Right now, Earth is birthing a new fifth-dimensional Golden Age, which will commence in 2032. We will see much change in our world for the highest good, and our hearts will be the driving force in the new era of love. It is important to act with integrity and take decisions that benefit not only the individual but humankind as a whole. We are moving from an ego-based civilization to a heart-based one. What we say, think, and do is helping to co-create the new age, so it is important to manifest and co-create the world you want to see.

Introducing Angels

What Are Angels?

Everyone has heard about angels, and people are connecting with them, especially now as Earth is moving into a higher dimension and more people are spiritually awake. Angels are highly evolved beings that reside from the seventh dimension onwards, and are also known as the messengers of Source. They are very pure and come from the heart of Source. Their will is aligned to the Divine, and they always act with unconditional love. From my experience, I know that if you open your heart to them, you will become aware that they are in continuous communication with you. They will leave you signs, and you will sense their loving presence.

Can I Talk to Angels?

Yes, you can. Raising your frequency, clearing your aura and opening your heart are important to form a close connection with the angels. These higher beings are associated with the Golden Ray of Angels. When you invoke it, the golden light soothes your aura and allows you to open up to the peace, love, and wisdom of these divine messengers. Just talk to the angels naturally, as you would with a friend, and you will be surprised by how they let you know they are present in your life.

Who Is My Guardian Angel?

I have been asked many times whether a deceased loved one would take on the task of acting as guardian angel. People like this idea, and it is true that your loved ones can become your guides. Still, they cannot become angels, because they are on a human pathway, going through reincarnations, whereas your guardian angel is part of the angelic realm. They have been assigned to you by Source and stay with you throughout all your lifetimes on Earth, other planets or universes, and in between, when you rest on the inner planes.

Your guardian angel holds the vision of your divine blueprint, and the bond between you is for eternity. They always stay at a short distance and step closer when you need them, and maybe whisper something into your ear or let a thought drop into your mind. Knowing your guardian angel's name strengthens your connection. You can find out your guardian angel's name through a visualization during this programme. As your guardian angel evolves with you over time, they may give you different names. My guardian angel was initially Henry, then Caeldron, and is now Wuji, a Chinese name. I asked one of my students living in China about its meaning, and she told me that it means "unlimited." I was amazed. Every time I say his name, I affirm that there are no limits to what I can do.

What Do Angels Look Like?

An angel can take any shape, and how they present themselves is unique to you. In your mind's eye or clairvoyantly, you may see them as a being of light with pure white wings or sense them as a sphere of coloured energy, or they will show themselves in another meaningful way. I usually sense a stream of angelic consciousness that comes down over me.

When I first consciously connected with my guardian angel, I saw him as a warrior angel, similar to the representations of Archangel Michael we are familiar with. It was the energy I needed to get through the tests that presented themselves in my life. As I was evolving, my guardian angel came in at a higher frequency, and it was quite a shock when he suddenly looked different. He was much brighter and luminous, wearing a pure white gown instead of the usual blue. His energy was more peaceful, as he was not displaying a sword, but I sensed that, if necessary, he would excel at wielding one. All in white, he was radiating the energy of an immortal divine being.

Are Angels Masculine or Feminine?

I have used "he" when writing about my guardian angel, because he presents himself with more masculine energy. In reality, however, angels have perfectly balanced masculine and feminine energies and are androgynous, so I have used gender-neutral "they" and "them" when speaking about guardian angels in general terms. You may perceive your angel as more masculine or feminine, depending on what serves you best. It resonates that I needed the male energy of the Warrior of Light.

Can I Ask Angels to Help Me?

Yes! Coming from the heart of Source, their love and compassion is beyond our comprehension. They are ready and willing to help you with anything. The key is that you must ask. If you don't ask, they will not intervene as they respect your free will. When I realized that there is always a response when I ask angels for help, it really boosted my faith. I trusted 100 percent that the angels would support me for the highest good whenever I asked. Results may not be instant, but the guidance is that you must look for signs after you have asked. As you go through this course, you will ask the angels to help you with various aspects of your home and life.

How Will I Know that Angels Are Helping Me?

Angels will leave you symbols, the most common being a white feather. When you see it, a realization, like a flash, will go through your mind that angels are with you. I used to live in an area with many birds, but I would always know when angels had left feathers to draw my attention to something. There are many other signs, such as angel clouds, reading or hearing the word "angel," or seeing a butterfly.

Birds are also messengers of angels, and if you tune in to their sound, you can get a message. I recently wrote an affirmative statement to help me enter deeper into my mission. The next day, I found a little label with the word "angels" attached to the paper where I had written my statement! I was blown away. What an incredible angel sign! I had intended for the label to go on a folder, and it ended up on this paper. I am sure it was no coincidence.

Are There Different Kinds of Angels?

Yes, **angels** vibrate at different frequencies in accordance with the work they carry out, but they are all equal, just as humans are all equal. There are angels for all aspects of life and anything you could imagine! There are angels of peace, wisdom, love, abundance, joy, computers, gardening, and so on. There are also parking angels if you need to find a parking space. Don't be shy; just ask. Angels love making your life easier.

Next are the **guardian angels**, which, as you already know, have the job of taking care of souls and helping them realize their highest potential. Guardian angels vibrate at a frequency that allows them to connect with you. They stay with you throughout your life and in between incarnations.

Then we have the higher-vibrational **archangels**, which serve in a cosmic capacity and oversee the guardian angels. They work in our universe and others, and more and more of them are stepping forward to assist Earth by making contact with lightworkers. Some of them have taken on the job of overlighting and activating the fifth-dimensional chakras for humanity, and you will learn more about this later in the book.

Principalities have the job of guarding on a larger scale. They oversee entire cities and nations and may even look after big companies and buildings such as schools. They also look after the many sacred-power sites around the world, such as temples and pyramids.

Powers, virtues, and **dominions** are on the next faster frequency band. **Powers** are highly illumined angels, including the angels of birth and death and the lords of karma, which oversee the Akashic records. **Virtues** beam huge columns of light containing wisdom codes to Earth. **Dominions** oversee the angelic realms below them that vibrate at a slower frequency.

The fastest-frequency angels are **thrones, cherubim,** and **seraphim**. They are graced by the light of Source, then step it down to levels we can safely absorb. **Thrones** are guardians of planets, and Lady Gaia is the ninth-dimensional throne in charge of Earth. **Cherubim** hold pure, transcendent love around stars and planets and are truly awesome angels. **Seraphim** are 12-dimensional angels known for surrounding the Godhead and singing *OM* to create His visions. Their essence is pure love, and they can birth stars and planets.

Do Angels Really Exist? A Personal Angel Story

When we ask angels to help us, it requires trust on our part—trust that they exist and trust that they will help.

Many years ago, when my three children were quite young, we walked through a park on our way home for lunch. It was the first Sunday of the month, and a market was taking place in our town. My eight-year-old daughter, Paulina, was misbehaving because I hadn't bought her something she wanted. I tried explaining that I didn't have the money to buy her a gift, not even money to do the food shopping the next day.

She wouldn't stop going on about it, and I felt quite desperate. Then I had an idea. I said to her, "Okay, let's try this. Let's ask our angels!" Together, we formulated a prayer: "Angels, please let us find some money so that we can buy presents and ice cream at the bar."

As soon as we walked out of the park gate, we saw a 50-euro note on the floor. We were overjoyed and thanked the angels. After lunch, I returned to the market with the children to buy them something of their choice. We had an ice cream, and there was even enough money left to buy food the next day. I was deeply grateful for this miraculous intervention by the angels, and it also left a deep impression on the children. Since that day, my youngest daughter (now 18 years old) has regularly asked me to make requests to the angels on her behalf.

Introducing Unicorns

What Are Unicorns?

Everyone knows unicorns as magical and mystical beings associated with enchanted forests. They have been represented in art throughout the ages, and we see them in movies and children's books. They are really making sure that we know they have returned in great numbers. More than ever, you see them as toys, clothing, and accessories for children and adults, but there is much more to unicorns than this. Unicorns are high-frequency beings, and they radiate purity.

Where Do Unicorns Live?

They are enlightened and reside from the seventh dimension upwards, just like angels. The higher the dimension, the more wondrous unicorns you can encounter with their special horns. Unicorns have been with us since Golden Atlantis, a golden era that lasted 1500 years. At the fall of Atlantis, the vibrations on Earth fell, and the unicorns withdrew to their stellar origin. With the rise in frequency on Earth, the unicorns are returning, and almost everyone knows about them because their representations are everywhere. This means that you can connect with them and their pure, sparkling, healing light.

How Can I Connect with Unicorns?

You can connect with your unicorns just as you can connect with your guardian angel. It is really easy. Just thinking about a unicorn will draw it to you. Many people are working with unicorns without being aware of it. Unicorns are attracted to children and people with pure hearts, pure intentions, and a desire to help others. Unicorns are also drawn to people with higher visions of helping others and the world – loving people who do not only think about themselves but have a passion for helping all of humanity, nature, and animals. Unicorns communicate with you through your soul and hold the vision of you realizing your soul's intentions for this lifetime.

How Can My Personal Unicorn Help Me?

Once you have connected with your unicorn, the bond remains, and your unicorn can greatly assist you with your enlightenment and evolving into a fifth-dimensional human. Your personal unicorn can help you embody your soul more fully and fulfil your highest destiny. The horn on a unicorn's brow is actually a spiral of light that it can use to transmit its energy to people and situations.

Introducing Dragons

What Are Dragons?

In Asian countries, dragons are considered auspicious, bringers of good fortune. They are an important part of the culture. You see them on temple walls, and being born in the year of the dragon is considered a lucky sign. The dragon is also a powerful feng shui symbol and a spiritual tool for clearing and balancing energies and empowering you. Dragons are in our consciousness in the West and the East because we "remember" them from the beginning of time. This is why we hear about them in legends, myths, and fairy tales. We see them on TV shows and in animations, and more and more lightworkers are now becoming aware of them. Since 2012, thousands of dragons have started returning to support Earth and humanity.

Lightworkers meditate and work with dragons and ask for guidance and help. Dragons, in reality, are elemental beings and belong to the angelic realms, just like angels and unicorns. They can be composed of fire, earth, air, water, and metal, and right now, even galactic dragons are assisting Earth and sharing their cosmic wisdom with us. Since 2015, the rising consciousness of the world has attracted them from their stellar homes, and they are bringing us the most awesome energies. The many, many dragons on Earth now are here to help us anchor the new Golden Age.

How Old Are Dragons?

Dragons have been around for aeons, and witnessed Earth's birth after it had been conceived in the mind of Source. They have been around to carry out specific tasks through the previous golden eras on Earth, such as Lemuria and Atlantis, and indeed, you may have worked with your dragon before in different lifetimes. In those times, dragons were fifth-dimensional or higher. Then, at the fall of Atlantis, the dragons made a sacrifice and dropped their frequency to 4D so they could carry on helping humanity. Dragons also helped create the leyline system on Earth, which is why these energy lines on our planet were originally called "dragon lines." Ley lines allowed pure spiritual energy to flow, and the areas where they intersected were used to build powerful sites. These ley lines are in need of clearing now.

Why Should I Make Friends with Dragons?

Dragons make wonderful companions and will protect you if asked. You have a personal dragon that stays with you throughout your incarnation. Your dragon can make your life so much easier and probably has a great sense of humour, but make sure you express gratitude as you would with human friends. You can ask your dragon anything and trust that it will carry out its mission. Dragons' speciality is to dissolve low and dense energies.

I have one dragon that accompanies me, but I know that some of my students have several. Daily communication and interaction are important, as is treating your dragon like a friend. You can talk to your dragon telepathically with your thoughts. One of my students, Yen Chi, has received a download from young dragons and can speak in dragon language with them. They appeared in our dragon classes because they wanted to learn about interaction with humans. Often, your dragon is the same element as your astrological sign. I am a fire sign, and my dragon has combined elements, fire and water, which fits my personality perfectly. I love water!

10 WEEKS TO TRANSFORM YOUR LIFE AND HOME

Seven Steps to Prepare for the Journey through the Bagua

STEP 1 – The Angel of Your Home

On the day I started writing this book, I had an amazing experience with the angel of my home. She appeared to me with a message. I sensed her as big with feminine energy, and she even dropped her name into my mind: Dora. She wanted me to use this name to interact with her. She told me that she would help me write this book and gave me the visualization for you to connect with your angel and find out their name.

The first step to raising the energies in your house or apartment is to connect with the angel of your home and ask them to overlight the transformation so it becomes a high-frequency space that attracts abundance in all its forms for you. You can definitely connect with the angel of your home because every habitation has one. Know that the angel will continue to work with you. Once you make the connection, they will remain, and the lighter and purer the energy in your home is, the easier it is for your angel to work with you and for you to have a deep relationship with them.

Note about the Angel of Your Home

Every building has an angel looking after it, whether it is an office, hospital, dentist's, shop, public building, castle, or private home. It is important to be aware that you affect the energy when you walk into a building. If you are a positive, happy, and peaceful person, you will contribute good energy to the space. This is service work, because you are making it easier for the angel of that building to connect with people and do their job. You are also helping people who work or live in the place to enjoy good energy.

Tips on How to Interact with the Angel of Your Home

- Sing for your angel with a smile on your face. Choose a high-frequency song or create your own tune and sing it from the heart.
- Chant the *OM* for the angel of your home. *OM* is the sound of creation, the most sacred sound of all sounds, and when you chant it, your consciousness reaches higher levels, allowing you to connect with the angel more easily.
- Once you find out your angel's name by doing the visualization below, you can also sing their name. That is a very powerful way to connect with them.
- Express gratitude by saying: "Angel of my home, I love you. Thank you for keeping the energies light and bright."
- Tell the angel of your home that you are committed to helping keep the energies high by being positive.
- Ask your guardian angel to speak with the angel of your home about how to support you in your evolution. Your guardian angel knows you best and holds the vision of your divine blueprint. So they can give the perfect advice.
- Be mindful of the angels of all buildings as you walk into them. Blessing the energy and greeting the angel make a huge difference.

VISUALIZATION to Connect with the Angel of Your Home

1. Close your eyes and get comfortable in your chair.
2. Send grounding roots deep into the earth.
3. Focus on your heart, and take a few deep and relaxing breaths.

4. Call the angel of your home, and ask them to come close.

5. As the angel enfolds you with their energy, you feel love and peace enter your heart.

6. Take time to interact with your angel and get a sense of their appearance.

7. Ask the angel to drop their name into your mind now.

8. Accept the name you were given. If you don't get a name, know that your angel will give it to you in the next few days. You might read or hear it somewhere and understand that this is it.

9. Ask the angel to help transform your home into a high-vibrational space that attracts abundance into your life.

10. Thank the angel for connecting with you and then open your eyes. Know that you have activated powerful help for your project, and the angel of your home will work with you.

STEP 2 – Activate Your Crystals to Work with You

Crystals are an extension of you and carry a consciousness and mission. They are multidimensional beings, and some are highly evolved, powerful beings. You can communicate with them because they are sentient beings. They guard ancient wisdom, and some originate from the stars. When you work with them, you are honouring them, and they are happy to share their wisdom with you. High-frequency crystals are at work to help Earth shift into the new Golden Age.

STEP 2 is to activate the crystals that reside in your home to work with you on a deeper level. A good time to do this is a day or two before the full moon. Put them outside in your garden or on a balcony or window sill. Let them cleanse and recharge under the moonlight, the sunlight, and the rain, being careful with crystals that might discolour in the sunlight, such as celestine or amethyst. Then bring the crystals back inside, and ask them to work with you actively. When I did this, the crystals suddenly came alive. I started putting them here and there and wore different crystal pendants. They would even come into my dreams and guide me on how to use them. I will give you more guidelines on how to work with them throughout the book.

Crystal Note

Crystals are associated with the first dimension. They evolve and live as they grow in the dark within the earth. Some of them are programmed with information, and they have healing properties. Each crystal has a crystal being, or *deva*, attached to it, which will leave the crystal once it has fulfilled its mission. Each crystal has different qualities; more lightworkers understand how special they are and work with them.

Many crystal books are readily available, but it's a good idea to tune in to your crystal and find out why it came to you. Each crystal in your possession has taken a journey to reach you, because it is the crystal that chooses you. It travels to you with the purpose of working with you for a common goal. Sharing their wonderful qualities with you is part of the crystals' mission. They also interact with each other.

Tips on How to Interact with Crystals

- Set the intention to connect with a stone or crystal and have a conversation.
- Bond with your crystal by holding it and looking at it from all angles, observing its colour variations and feeling its shape.
- Tune into the crystal's qualities, and discover why it came to you. What is it here to help you with?
- Hold a rose quartz crystal, and ask it to connect with all rose quartz in your surroundings and within the earth, creating a powerful network that emanates the divine qualities of love and compassion.
- Hold an amethyst crystal, and ask it to connect with all amethyst crystals in your surroundings and within the earth, creating a powerful network that emanates the quality of transmutation.

EXERCISE to Programme a Crystal to Help You Transform Your Home

1. Choose one crystal intuitively.
2. Hold it to your heart and say: "Beloved crystal, I now set your frequency to the fifth dimension and beyond."
3. Allow the crystal to set at this frequency.
4. Say: "Beloved crystal, thank you for coming to me and helping me raise my frequency and that of my home."
5. Keep it near you, trusting that it supports you with transforming your home into a fifth-dimensional space and bringing flow into your life.

EXERCISE to Ask a Network of Rose Quartz Crystals to Stream Love into Your Home

1. Hold a rose quartz crystal and ask it to connect with all rose quartz crystals in your building and surroundings. If you live in a high-rise building with many apartments, your crystal will connect with any other rose quartz in the same or nearby buildings. It will also connect to the rose quartz crystals within the earth in your part of the world.
2. Sense this happening, creating a powerful network that emanates the divine qualities of love, compassion, caring, kindness, gentleness, and cooperation for the highest good.
3. Ask the network of rose quartz crystals to stream these beautiful divine qualities into your building and home. Sit in silence while this is happening, enjoying the sensations.
4. When the work is complete, remember to thank the crystals.

STEP 3 – Clear the Space below
Your Home with an Earth Dragon

Low energies below your home may impact the frequency of vibration in your home and, therefore, your life, so it is very important to clear them. When you remove limiting energies below your building, more supportive light can enter your living space, positively affecting you and creating space for new, exciting things to enter your life. Because of the sacrifice dragons made at the fall of Atlantis, they can work in very dense areas and clear the lowest energies that angels cannot reach. Their mission is to prepare humans and the planet for the new high-frequency energies.

You will work with an earth dragon to purify the energies below your home. As with all higher beings, you must ask first and then they will happily help you.

Earth Dragon Note

As the frequency of our planet rises, the wise earth dragons wake up. They are fourth-dimensional, appear in all shades of brown, and their light contains the love and wisdom codes of Source. They are also lighting up the wisdom contained within the crystals that have been placed into the earth aeons ago, at the time of Lemuria. One special ability and task of earth dragons is to travel along the ley lines to clear lower energies. It is service work to instruct earth dragons to do this. It has a great and positive influence on the land and people, especially if you clear the energy below habitations or places where many people gather.

Tips on How to Interact with an Earth Dragon

- Ask an earth dragon to help you ground, and it will happily do so. You can imagine it below your feet, anchoring your energy into the earth.
- Ask an earth dragon to clear the energies below your home or workplace.

- Ask a legion of earth dragons to delve into the planet and clear the ley lines of your country or the whole world.
- Say a prayer to honour the earth dragons. For example:

> *"Dear earth dragons, thank you for awakening and helping to clear the earth from lower energies. I send you my love and gratitude."*

> *"Dear earth dragons, thank you for clearing the earth below my home. I love you, I thank you, I bless you, and I honour you."*

> *"Dear earth dragons, thank you for keeping me grounded and safe while I am driving. I love you."*

VISUALIZATION to Clear the Energies below Your Home with an Earth Dragon

1. Close your eyes and relax.
2. Invoke a brown earth dragon, visualize it delving deep into the earth below your home, and ask it to clear any lower energies.
3. See the dragon blazing fire and carrying out this task. You can assist by visualizing the energies flowing freely and pure light spreading below your home.
4. Thank the dragon for its help.

STEP 4 – Clear the Space that Contains Your Home with Dragons and Angels

We will use sacred geometry, angels, and gold and silver violet flame dragons to help you clear the space that contains your home. The violet flame of transmutation is a powerful tool to heal on all levels. The added silver brings grace and harmony, and the gold brings wisdom. Make it a habit to do the short visualization daily as you work through this book. It only takes a minute and is very efficient.

Gold and Silver Violet Flame Dragon Note

The magnificent gold and silver violet flame dragons can transmute any lower old energies with their blazing flames. They can help you release traumatic events from your current incarnation, past lifetimes, and all that no longer serves you by etherically burning it up and replacing it with new joyful and light energy. They work with Archangel Zadkiel, the angel of transmutation, and Ascended Master St. Germain. These dragons protect you when you work with them, and they lighten you up. As you clear energies in yourself or your home, miracles can happen.

Tips on How to Interact with the Gold and Silver Violet Flame Dragons

- You can invoke gold and silver violet dragons simply by calling them and giving them instructions. For example:

    "I invoke the gold and silver violet flame dragons to clear my space."

    "I invoke the gold and silver violet flame dragons to clear my path."

    "I invoke the gold and silver violet flame dragons to fill me with joy."

- You can set the intention to befriend a gold and silver violet dragon. Simply call one and communicate with it. Ask if it's okay to keep calling on it to help you clear your energies and feel more joyful.

VISUALIZATION to Clear the Energies around Your Home with Angels and Dragons

1. Close your eyes and relax.
2. Invoke a pyramid from the heavens to come down and be placed over your building. This pyramid is blazing with gold, silver, and violet light. Invoke an upside-down

pyramid from the centre of the earth to rise and form a sacred geometric double pyramid or octahedron around your building.

3. See the gold and silver violet flame dragons flying within your pyramid, blazing gold and silver violet flames to clear the energies and create a high-frequency space. See angels of joy flying around this sacred shape, singing. Their celestial tunes raise the frequencies as high as possible to support you with your work.

4. Thank the angels and dragons.

STEP 5 – Declutter with Your Home Transformation Team

Life is a continuous cycle of letting go of the old and replacing it with new, higher energies. The old can be clutter, but also thoughts and beliefs that block you. The speed at which you replace what no longer serves you depends on you. This section aims to make you think about the flow of your life. When you hoard things in your home, you can block the flow of your life. All you see around you is energy, and energy should flow. This is a universal law. Is your life flowing, or is it stagnating? When you clear your stuff, the energies can flow freely. It can drag you down and deplete your forces if you have too many things. The energy and objects in your home affect your physical, emotional, mental, and spiritual bodies.

Clearing clutter, therefore, has incredible benefits. It can:

- Energize and revitalize you
- Have a positive impact on your health
- Make you feel enthusiastic and motivated
- Bring you clarity and positivity
- Bring you order and structure
- Make your home more beautiful and high frequency
- Move you more deeply into your life mission.

When you purchased this book, you demonstrated your intention to transform your home and life to the Universe. As you read through the book and do the exercises, the energies will inevitably start moving. You will find yourself clearing clutter. The higher beings guiding you will push you to clear out the bathroom cabinet, kitchen cupboard, wardrobe, and so on. You will find yourself taking trips to dispose of all the excess you have accumulated.

I noticed that it was contagious: when I started clearing, my daughter did the same. She had already done it before I had time to sort out the bathroom cabinet. She literally forced me to sort out my wardrobe and the drawer beneath my bed. So your family members will probably join you when they see you doing it. I also noticed that when I teach a class with content from this book, it has the same effect: I will start clearing out stuff. You may also wish to consult the last chapter of the book, Serious Decluttering.

Now we will call the higher beings guiding you for this project. They are your "Home Transformation Team." Your Home Transformation Team includes the angel of your home, your guardian angel, your personal unicorn and dragon, and other higher beings that already support you or you will meet as you read on. For now, just bring to your awareness that you have a team that helps you transform your home and life.

INVOKE Your Home Transformation Team

1. Close your eyes and relax.
2. Invoke your Home Transformation Team, and feel their presence, the angel of your home, your guardian angel, your personal unicorn and dragon, and other higher beings that are perfect for you and your home.
3. Tell them about your intention to transform your home and life, and ask them for guidance.
4. Listen to their response.
5. Feel gratitude in your heart, and thank them.

STEP 6 – The 5D Bagua of Higher Aspirations

The Chinese bagua (bāguà 八卦) is an energetic map that guides the application of feng shui in a space. *Bagua* means "eight symbols" and refers to eight divinatory trigrams, also known as "the Eight Aspirations." Traditionally, it is represented as an octagon with eight sections surrounding the centre called *taiji* (tàijí 太极), or the yin-yang symbol representing harmony. *Taiji* means "supreme ultimate" in ancient Chinese cosmology, presented as the primary source of all created things.

When the Eight Aspirations are met, the result is *taiji*, representing perfect harmony. Each section's *yin* (feminine) or *yang* (masculine) energy is represented by a series of three parallel lines, either broken or unbroken. The solid ones represent yang, and the broken ones represent yin, and are linked to a family member, such as the father or the eldest son, because they symbolize a type of energy.

The bagua is also called the Magic Luoshu Square, the Scroll of Luo River, or the Yellow River Map. The following is a lovely legend about how the Magic Luoshu Square was gifted to the people:

It was a time of great floods in 650 BC, when the Luo River overflowed and inundated people's dwellings. They rushed to pray and make offerings to the river god to calm his anger so he would return the water to its normal level, when suddenly a magic turtle emerged from beneath the waters.

It had a curious grid of nine squares on its shell, and dots adding up to numbers within each square. When the circular dots in this three-by-three grid are added diagonally, vertically, or horizontally, the sum is always 15.

The number 15 corresponds to the number of days in the new moon cycle to the full moon in the 14 cycles of the Chinese solar year. The odd numbers carry yang energy, the divine masculine, while the even numbers carry yin energy, the divine feminine. An ancient Chinese master understood that patterns on the turtle's back were a map of the natural energy flow and universal laws.

In this way, the bagua became a fundamental tool in the feng shui tradition. It was originally used for city planning and tomb design, but became very popular in the West because it is a wonderful, simple tool to create a harmonious environment.

The 5D Bagua of Higher Aspirations we will be working with is also known as the Later Heaven Bagua, which is attributed to King Wen. In the layout below, Kan (water) is at the bottom, and Li (fire) is at the top. It is a dynamic bagua, in which the energies from each area are interconnected and flow from one area to the next.

Each area of the 5D Bagua of Higher Aspirations is related to a part of your home and an aspect of your life and has layers of meaning:

Square 1 traditionally represents your career;

square 2, your relationships;

square 3, your family;

square 4, your wealth;

square 5, your health;

square 6, helpful people;

square 7, children;

square 8, knowledge; and

square 9, fame.

I tuned into the higher aspects of the bagua for this book and developed keywords and colours for each square. I am calling it "5D Bagua of Higher Aspirations" as the intention is to help you align with your fifth-dimensional possibilities and prepare you for the new Golden Age.

You can apply it to the whole floor plan, an individual room, a desk, or any space, even a city. To easily apply the bagua to a floor plan, you can draw it as a square divided into nine smaller squares of the same size. The numbers are powerful and are an expression of specific energies. We will connect with them as we work in each area.

5D Bagua of Higher Aspirations

Xun WIND *'Open up to Abundance'* 4	**Li** FIRE *'Your True Magnificence'* 9	**Kun** EARTH *'Your Beautiful Open Heart'* 2
Zhen THUNDER *'The Gifts of Your Ancestors'* 3	**Taiji** ☯ *'Balance and Glorious Health'* 5	**Dui** LAKE *'Never-ending Creativity'* 7
Gen MOUNTAIN *'Embody Your Soul and Access its Wisdom'* 8	**Kan** WATER *'Your Life Mission'* 1	**Qian** HEAVEN *'Incredible Higher Support'* 6

Square 1	Kǎn	Water	Your Life Mission
Square 2	Kūn	Earth	Your Beautiful Open Heart
Square 3	Zhèn	Thunder	The Gifts of Your Ancestors
Square 4	Xùn	Wind	Open up to Abundance
Square 5	Tàijí	Centre	Balance and Glorious Health
Square 6	Qián	Heaven	Incredible Higher Support
Square 7	Duì	Lake	Never-Ending Creativity
Square 8	Gèn	Mountain	Embodying Your Soul and Accessing its Wisdom
Square 9	Lí	Fire	Your True Magnificence

DRAW Your Bagua

It is very easy to draw your bagua if you already have a floor plan for your house or apartment. Take a copy and then impose the bagua map upon it by dividing it into nine squares (or rectangles, depending on the measurements of your floor plan).

The bottom line of the bagua, square numbers 8, 6, and 1 (see the image), aligns with the main entrance to your home. So measure the floor plan—let's say it is 30 cm long; divide it by three, and the result is 10. Then take the width of your apartment—let's say it is 21 cm, so you divide it by 3, and the result is 7. You can thus draw your nine squares, each measuring 10 x 7 cm.

If you haven't got the floor plan, you can measure each room and create it yourself. All you need is a measuring tape, ruler, pen, and paper. After you have drawn the plan, divide it into nine squares.

STEP 7 – The Entrance to Your Home

Your entrance is probably part of one of the bagua areas, but we will give it special attention because it is where good energy can enter your home. It should be clear and tidy and supported with items that can raise the vibration of the energy flow. I have a beautiful, decorative black-golden umbrella stand here—interestingly, umbrellas symbolize protection. There is a blue coat rack on the wall, from which coloured scarves are hanging and a violet butterfly. The scarf colours are pink, violet, magenta, lilac red, orange, yellow, green, blue, turquoise, black, white, and silver. All colours have qualities, and the flow of energy will spread their qualities throughout your home. The butterfly is a symbol of transformation. On page 42, I am also sharing a 5D colour chart, which you may find useful for transforming your home.

I feel that wind chimes are essential in this area, and the ones I bought look ancient Chinese and have golden bells. On a windy day, they chime beautifully when I have the window open. When that happens, I feel blessed and sense that something magical is unfolding. They purify the energy that comes through here. On the wall beside the door, there is a decorative heart. I asked my angel of the home to bless it, and I set the intention for this heart to open up the hearts of people who come through here and surround them with a pink sphere of fifth-dimensional love. I have also asked Archangel Michael to place one of his angels here for protection. Read the information below to connect with Archangel Michael's powerful light, and then have a look at your entrance and reflect on whether there is anything you can do to facilitate the flow of *qi* (chi).

Meet Archangel Michael

Archangel Michael is the angel of protection, appearing in a glorious royal blue light. He radiates power, courage, and strength and is usually depicted as a warrior angel holding the Sword of Truth and the Blue Shield of Protection. You can call on Archangel Michael to protect and empower you and cut any cords or attachments with his sword. He is in charge of developing the throat chakra for humanity at a fifth-dimensional level to facilitate higher communication. He has his spiritual retreat at Lake Louise in Banff, Canada, which you can visit in meditation or sleep to receive his teachings by simply setting the intention. His twin flame is Archangel Faith.

Tips on How to Interact with Archangels Michael and Faith

- You can connect with Archangel Michael by simply saying or thinking his name.
- You may wish to sing his name, which is a beautiful way of honouring him and establishing a connection.
- Say this prayer to protect your entrance area: "Beloved Archangel Michael, please place one of your angels at my entrance to protect it 24 hours a day. Thank you with all my heart."
- To increase your communication skills, you can say: "Beloved Archangel Michael, please touch my throat chakra so I can speak my truth easily and lovingly." Then, feel his touch on your throat; the chakra expands with beautiful royal blue light.

- You can ask Archangel Michael to send his legions of angels to protect people all over the world.
- Ask Archangel Michael to wrap you into his deep blue cloak of protection and then see and feel it all around you.
- Ask Archangel Michael to empower you with his divine masculine energy and feel power, courage, and strength flow into you. This is very useful when you have a difficult task to master.
- Use a blue sapphire to connect with Archangel Michael. The sapphire is Archangel Michael's energy solidified.
- Ask Archangel Faith to fill you with the highest faith, so you can trust the Universe to look after you.

5D Colour Chart	
Brown	the colour of the earth, grounds you.
Black	is associated with the safety of the womb and the divine feminine. It is a protective and mysterious colour.
White	contains all colours and is associated with deep purification and the purity of the heart.
Silver	is associated with the divine feminine and helps you to ground and create a solid foundation.
Platinum	is associated with joy and feeling secure.
Pink	is the colour of love, compassion, and an open heart.
Orange	is a warm, welcoming colour associated with your passions, life purpose, and oneness.
Red	stands for dynamic action and stepping into your power.
Yellow	is a joyful colour.
Gold	is associated with wisdom and, in Feng shui, attracts abundance.
Blue	is associated with higher communication and also with the flow of water and the heavens.
Green	is the colour of healing and abundance.
Magenta	is the colour of higher love and the wisdom of your soul.

KAN – Your Life Mission

BAGUA AREA 1

Area 1 of the bagua is called Kan. The energy of Kan is yin/yang/yin and is associated with the energy of the middle son: study, vitality, independence, and uniqueness. Kan symbolizes water, and its element is also water. Bringing the element of water into the area is beneficial. Kan traditionally represents your career and the life path you walk in this life. For our purposes, on my 5D Bagua of Higher Aspirations, I have called it Your Life Mission.

I have given this bagua area the colour white. I associate white with Archangel Gabriel, the angel of purity, who can illuminate the keys and codes of your mission in your aura, and the unicorns, whose job is to align you with your soul mission. I felt white was the perfect colour to align you more deeply with your life purpose. Also, white contains all the other colours and all their qualities.

Your personal mission is the reason why you are here on Earth right now. Before you incarnated, your soul met with your guardian angel, your overlighting archangel and other higher beings that work with you, and together, you decided what you wanted to learn and achieve in this lifetime. Achieving your life mission is achieving your highest destiny. Depending on where you are in your evolution, you may still wonder what your life purpose is, or you may already be deeply engaged in your soul mission. When you are aligned with your soul intentions you know it, because you get up with enthusiasm in your heart and feel motivated to carry out your work.

When I discovered that my life mission square falls into the main bathroom and the corridor, I first thought, *Hmm*, but I always see the positive side. A bathroom is a place for purification and elimination and a place where water flows. However, the bathroom is not the place to activate your life mission or any other bagua area. I was pleased when I looked at my corridor because the energy could flow freely. There is nothing there, no obstruction, and the only decoration is one beautiful blue-green seahorse, which reminds me of the oceans. Water is a symbol of flow, so it is perfect for my life mission, which I am in the process of activating at a higher level.

In this chapter, you will meet some more members of your Home Transformation Team, particularly a water dragon with the power to clear the area for you. The level of success of this energetic work depends on your commitment. When you activate your life mission, the energy will flow, and things will happen in your life. There will be signs and synchronicities. Are you willing to listen and take action? To move forward, you have to act. But now, please read the information about the water dragons, then check out your Kan area, and let's clear it.

Water Dragon Note

As the name suggests, water dragons are connected with the element of water and reside in it. Water is a carrier for cosmic love and the Christ light, which the dragons spread through their beautiful open hearts. They are fourth-dimensional beings and are a gentle green colour like water. Just as they glide through the water with their serpent-like bodies, they can help you easily flow around obstacles or challenges while maintaining an open heart. They can also help you develop your intuition and psychic abilities. Water dragons carry the qualities of grace and harmony. Unlike other dragons, water dragons cannot breathe fire!

Tips on How to Interact with a Water Dragon

- If you live near the sea or a lake, befriend the water dragons that live in your area. You can do this with intention and by simply calling out to them and saying hello.

- When you bathe or swim, you can ask the water dragons to fill the water with love.
- Water dragons can fill you with love because your cells contain water. Try the following invocation: "Beloved water dragon, please send love through my cells."
- When you need to make a decision, you can say: "Beloved water dragon, please reinforce my intuition so I can choose easily." Then, tune into it and decide with your heart.
- If you need to bring harmony into your relationships, you can say: "Beloved water dragon, please help me treat people kindly and find the right words when I speak with them."
- If you feel something is blocking you, you can say: "Beloved water dragon, please help me flow around the obstacle." Say thank you, and trust that the water dragon is helping you.
- Imagine gliding through the waters in the company of a water dragon. You may wish to imagine yourself as a mermaid and just have fun together.
- Always remember to be grateful and thank the water dragons for their help.

VISUALIZATION to Clear the Kan Area with a Water Dragon

1. Sit in the space that represents your life mission.
2. Light a candle and burn some incense.
3. Set the intention to raise the energy and activate your life mission at a higher level.
4. Call your angel of the home to be present and overlight this work. You may wish to ask your guardian angel to come close. Remember, your guardian angel is your most loyal companion and holds the vision of your divine soul blueprint. They know who you truly are and love you unconditionally.

5. Visualize the area filling with pure, magical, clear water. Be creative. See and hear waterfalls cascading down the walls. Sense how refreshing this is and know that water carries love.

6. See a most graceful, gentle, green water dragon moving through the water, purifying the space with light emanating from its beautiful shimmering body and mouth. It is filling the water with cosmic love.

7. While the water dragon is cleaning and spreading love, reflect on whether you need to do anything else in this area. Should you remove or add things? You can have a conversation with the water dragon and ask it for advice.

8. Thank the dragon for its insights and cleansing.

9. Bring back your consciousness into your physical body.

Unicorns

Think about whether you want to activate your life mission in another room. Remember that you can also apply the entire bagua to one room. You may have a high-frequency room in your home where you feel it would be beneficial to activate it. My high-frequency space is the living room, where I meditate. I was pleasantly surprised when I checked where the bagua area for my life mission falls. It was the middle of my long library full of crystals and high-frequency books.

To my amazement, I had placed several unicorns exactly in this part of the library. Unicorns are perfect because it is their job to help you align with your soul mission, and they will automatically be attracted to you when you start thinking and focusing on your mission.

Next to my unicorns, I have selenite crystals, which connect you with unicorns. Clear quartz crystals will amply and magnify anything, so if you can get hold of unicorns, I recommend putting them in your life mission area. Beautiful unicorns made of crystal are available, and you may wish to purchase one. Please read the information about personal unicorns before doing the visualization to meet your unicorn and find out its name.

Personal Unicorn Note

When I met my personal unicorn many years ago, he appeared as an elderly white male horse, a bit stocky and not very tall. He had a horn of light, and the name he gave me was Ezeriah. I associated him with wisdom. When he appeared, I was filled with excitement and joy.

Ezeriah made things happen for me. A few days later, a friend who ran a spiritual centre asked me to do a workshop about unicorns. I immediately suspected that Ezeriah had something to do with this.

I was not a good speaker at the time. I was very shy and introverted, but my philosophy was to do things, especially if they scared me. Of course, I recognized it as a golden opportunity, and in fact, it set me on my path as a spiritual teacher, because that was my mission and destiny. In more recent times, when teaching a course on Lemurian healing, Ezeriah appeared to me in a much more ethereal form, looking younger and full of grace, and what struck me most were his clear and bright eyes.

When I first met Ezeriah, I assumed he would be my only unicorn, but then I discovered that this was not true. On an Atlantis training, I invited my students to invoke their personal unicorns during visualization. I expected Ezeriah to show up for me, but a completely different unicorn appeared. He looked much bigger than a usual horse and told me his name was Simsa. When he saw that I was surprised by his presence, he told me that he was my Atlantean unicorn.

What stood out most about him was his aura of power and strength, and I realized he was helping me step more into my power while I was facilitating this course, a confirmation that we are never alone! We always have a team of helpers with us. One of my students, who is clairvoyant, reported that he could see a big unicorn behind me. There was much excitement, laughter, and bonding in the group when we discovered that we could have more than one unicorn.

Later on, Sarah appeared during a unicorn training. She called herself a ninth-dimensional diamond unicorn and appeared with sparkling diamonds in her lustrous white mane. She explained that these pure gems bring purity to the world. These enlightened unicorns can use powerful diamonds to cut away from your energy fields all that no longer serves you.

Sarah is so beautiful that I find it impossible to put it into words. She is pure love and pure grace. Her mane was laid out so beautifully that usually I say that she looked like she had been to the hairdresser. The diamond unicorns have an etheric retreat on Mount Shasta and work with Archangel Gabriel to bring purity to humanity during this time of great change.

After meeting my third unicorn, it became obvious to me that each of them had their own unique, outstanding, divine qualities: power, love, and wisdom. These three happen to be the qualities of the first three of the divine rays that Source beams to Earth, representing the most important of His aspects that He wishes us to absorb in a balanced way. Power always needs to be balanced with love and wisdom so you can use it for the highest good.

What Can Your Unicorn Do for You?

- Your unicorn will miraculously turn up to support you when you start thinking about your life mission.
- Your unicorn will help you manifest your dreams for the highest good of all.
- Your unicorn will nudge you in the right direction and pour ideas and higher inspirations into your mind—it can literally nudge your shoulder like a horse does.
- Your unicorn can fill you with the confidence to fulfil your mission and the knowing that you make a difference to our planet.
- Your unicorn can offer guidance on starting and completing projects. A special unicorn may come to work with you on a specific project, and when the project is finished, it will leave.
- Your unicorn can heal and enlighten you.

Tips on How to Interact with Your Personal Unicorn

- Say a prayer to help you manifest your life mission: "Beloved unicorn, please use your silver-white light to clear away any illusions I may hold so that my soul mission becomes visible and manifests fully into my life." Or say: "Beloved unicorn, please help me to embody my soul more fully and manifest my highest destiny."
- Ask your unicorn to take you flying, then imagine yourself riding on its back over tree tops and breathtaking nature with mountains and valleys and little waterfalls tumbling down. This is empowering and fills you with the quality of freedom.
- Selenite crystal can help you connect with unicorns. Hold such a crystal, or connect with an etheric one. Then call out to your unicorn, and ask it to wrap you in its magical, pure white light.
- Ask your unicorn to enlighten you, and see it pouring light from its horn into your third eye.
- Visualize your unicorn walking through your home, into every room, and spreading white light with gold and silver sparkles to bring magic into your life and space.
- In the presence of your unicorn, affirm: "I know my potential is limitless because my unicorn supports my dreams."
- You can sing your unicorn's name.

VISUALIZATION to Meet Your Personal Unicorn and Receive Its Name

1. Close your eyes and relax.
2. Invoke pure white unicorn light to come into your space, and breathe it in. Focus on your breath. Breathe the unicorn light in and out into your aura. With each breath you take, you become more and more relaxed.
3. Call your unicorn, and ask it to come close. Feel its loving presence and pure energy. Observe your unicorn. Does it have masculine or feminine energies? Look into its eyes and make a soul-to-soul connection. What colour are its eyes?
4. If this is the first time you have consciously connected with your unicorn, you may wish to find out its name. Ask your unicorn to drop its name into your mind now. Accept whatever name you are given, and trust it is the right vibration for connecting and working with your personal unicorn.
5. Your unicorn's job is to help you align with your soul's intentions. Know that your unicorn will stay close from now on and guide you deeper and deeper into your life mission. Thank your unicorn for its support.
6. Feel your feet firmly on the ground, and open your eyes.

Meet Archangel Gabriel

Archangel Gabriel is the Angel of Purity, and he appears with a pure white shimmering aura. He radiates purity and joy and can bring order and clarity into your life and guide your next steps and life mission. When you connect with his energy, everything becomes crystal clear and you feel secure and uplifted. He is in charge of developing the base, sacral, and navel chakras for humanity at a fifth-dimensional level. Archangel Gabriel has spiritual retreats above Mount Shasta in Northern California and at Findhorn in Scotland. His cosmic diamond can cut away and dissolve lower energies, emotions, or beliefs. His twin flame is Archangel Hope.

Tips on How to Interact with Archangels Gabriel and Hope

- You can connect with Archangel Gabriel simply by thinking, saying, or singing his name, thereby inviting his energy into your home.
- You can ask Archangel Gabriel and his pure white angels to radiate the white light of purity through your home or the world and visualize this happening.
- If you are unsure about making a decision, call Archangel Gabriel and ask him to wrap you in his white light to bring clarity.
- You can say this prayer: "Beloved Archangel Gabriel, I pray for deep purification and clarity about my next step. Thank you."
- You can ask your spirit to visit Archangel Gabriel's spiritual retreat at night when you sleep to receive deep purification and clarity. Do this with intention and say the words: "My spirit is visiting Archangel Gabriel's retreat tonight."
- Invoke Archangel Gabriel and ask him to fill your heart with divine joy.
- Call upon Archangel Gabriel to inspire you with divine creativity.
- If you have a diamond, you can use it to connect with Archangel Gabriel. The diamond is the Archangel Gabriel's energy solidified.
- Invoke Archangel Hope, and ask her to surround you with rainbow light and fill you with hope, excitement, and inspiration for your next steps.

VISUALIZATION to Activate Your Life Mission with the Diamond Unicorns

1. Close your eyes and relax.
2. Call your personal unicorn to come close. It will accompany you on a journey. Set the intention to activate your life mission at a higher level before you set off.

3. With your unicorn, take yourself to a beautiful nature spot with majestic pine trees and wildflowers. You are leaning against a tree, breathing in the fresh air and fragrant scents. Breathe love into your heart.

4. You can see a snowy mountain cap in the distance and a beautiful clear spring of flowing crystalline water with a cascading waterfall before you.

5. The most amazing thing happens. Seven graceful, pure white unicorns emerge from the trees and approach the spring. They lower their heads to drink. When they have finished, they raise their gaze and look directly at you. Yes, the unicorns have been expecting you.

6. Walk towards the unicorns. One of them telepathically welcomes you and tells you that they are ninth-dimensional diamond unicorns. They are a group of healing unicorns that have come to help you align with your soul intentions.

7. The unicorn invites you to look into the water. Suddenly, the smooth surface begins to ripple, and you see the shimmering body of a beautiful water dragon emerge. The loving energy coming from this dragon is so strong that you feel your own heart centre respond, sending love to it. You know that this water dragon is a high-frequency being that loves you tremendously. It telepathically invites you to come into the water for a swim.

8. You joyously agree and enter the water. It is the perfect temperature for you, and very refreshing. Take some time to enjoy yourself and have fun. Swim with the dragon and explore the waters. You may wish to ride on the dragon's back. Venture to the waterfalls, and let it cascade down on you to purify your energy fields on all levels. Take some time for this.

9. You feel pure and revitalized now. The dragon accompanies you to the shore, where the unicorns are

waiting. You are now ready to receive healing. The unicorns invite you to lie down comfortably. They stand around you in a circle and direct energy from their horns into your aura. You might see different types of energy emerge from their horns: pearlescent white, diamond white, sparkling silver or gold, or other colours. Etheric diamonds are working on you, removing crystallizations from your energy fields.

10. While the unicorns carry out their work, meditate on the following questions: What are your dreams? What activities bring you deep satisfaction? Take a few minutes for this, and come up with three things for each question.

11. The unicorns take a step back now, and you stand up. Suddenly, you are aware of the presence of a mighty being. Archangel Gabriel himself is standing before you. He welcomes you warmly as you gaze into his eyes with awe. He explains that he can light up the symbols and codes in your aura to activate your life mission at a higher level.

12. Archangel Gabriel raises his hands to comb through your energy fields. Your life mission is encoded in your aura, and your bodies of light consist of fire letters. Wherever Archangel Gabriel touches a symbol or code related to your purpose, it lights up beautifully. Your aura is radiating with high-frequency keys and codes now. It is a truly stunning sight.

13. Archangel Gabriel asks you a question: "What have you come to do here on Earth?" Take a moment to respond. Whatever your answer is, Archangel Gabriel blesses it.

14. It is time to return. Thank Archangel Gabriel and the diamond unicorns for the healing and insights you have received so that you can radiate more light.

15. With your personal unicorn, walk back through the woods. Hear the birds singing their messages. They are praising your magnificence.

16. Together with your personal unicorn, return safely into your own space and feel grounded.

Take some time to reflect upon how you have answered the questions and think about the actions you can take to express your soul's essence consciously. It is why you are incarnated on Earth right now.

The Power of Numbers and the Cosmic Turtle

In traditional feng shui, the principle of the nine numbers is that you are surrounded by different kinds of *qi* (chi) associated with the directions and the way the sun affects Earth. We will take this to a higher level and look at the cosmic origin of numbers.

All numbers are energy and form a pool of ninth-dimensional light somewhere in the cosmos. They are a tool for higher understanding and accelerating your ascension path. Stepped down, they still impact you, but when you connect with them at a universal level, they have a very powerful effect and transmit divine qualities.

Each week, you are invited to do a short visualization to journey to these ninth-dimensional pools and connect with a different number in the company of a cosmic turtle.

The Cosmic Turtle

Remember the story about the magic turtle that emerged from the Luo River with a grid of nine squares on her shell and dots adding up to numbers? Turtles are highly evolved and pure beings from another universe. They radiate cosmic abundance, including love, happiness, prosperity, enlightenment, and peace. Turtles, since ancient times, have symbolized immortality, longevity, and tenacity, because they get very old. In feng shui, the turtle represents wisdom, endurance and long life. We will work with this powerful symbol. The magic cosmic turtle will accompany you on the journey to the ninth-dimensional cosmic pool and add its energy to the number's vibration to magnify the outcome.

Connect with the Number One

The number one is about who you truly are, your individuality, and accessing your unique gifts. It also brings you leadership qualities, ambition, and dynamism and provides the force that moves you forward. It is a masculine energy.

1. Visualize the turtle rising from the Luo River water. Fascinated, you observe the map on its back. The area with one dot is illuminated.
2. As you observe the glowing dot, you find yourself transported onto the back of the turtle, and it floats up to the cosmic ninth-dimensional pool of the number one in the midst of stars and planets.
3. The turtle lands in the pool, and the energy streams into you, bathing you with the divine qualities you need to accomplish your mission.
4. Absorb and integrate leadership qualities, ambition, dynamism, and the force that moves you forward, knowing who you truly are and accessing your unique gifts.
5. Thank the turtle for the gifts it brought you, and return to your room.

Intention for the Kan Area of Your Life

"I stand in my power and fulfil my destiny."

Intentions are very powerful. This intention and affirmation dropped into my mind for this area. You may wish to write your own, or you can use my affirmation daily in the coming week.

KUN – Your Beautiful Open Heart

BAGUA AREA 2

This area of your bagua is called Kun. The energy of the Kun area is yin/yin/yin, and it is associated with the mother. Kun symbolizes earth and its element is also earth, which immediately conjures up the image of Mother Earth, who nurtures you lovingly. Kun traditionally represents your relationships. For our purposes, on my 5D Bagua of Higher Aspirations, I have called it Your Beautiful Open Heart.

I have given this bagua area the colour pink. I associate pink with the Archangel Chamuel, the angel of love, in charge of the heart centre and the divine feminine qualities of love and compassion. I felt pink is the perfect colour to open your heart to higher love and heal your relationship.

Kun is about being receptive, opening your heart, giving and receiving love, and motherhood. It is the purest form of yin energy, the divine feminine, which includes love, compassion, togetherness, cooperation, and caring. When your heart is open, you become receptive, and good things can enter your life. When your heart is open, it becomes beautiful, like a pure white lotus flower with love flowing from its petals.

When your heart is open, you can easily heal all your relationships. Right now, we are asked to operate from the heart. Love is the most powerful force and can dissolve any lower energies. This area is also about your relationships with your partner and other people, but also the relationship you have with yourself and Source. With the shift of energies, all relationship problems come to the surface to be healed, and forgiveness is required to move forward. You are encouraged to view all your relationships with the eyes of love. Archangel Chamuel can help heal relationships and open your heart, and we can also work with the goddess Kuan Yin.

I discovered that the Kun area is almost completely missing from my home. The only bit covering it is a tiny corner in the kitchen where I casually placed some paper bags, and part of it falls in my daughter's room. I removed the paper bags and affixed wind chimes to the ceiling. The wind chimes are in the shape of a half moon with two love birds sitting on it and a heart behind them. They bring movement and activate the energy to flow and spread throughout the space.

I then sat in the tiny corner of my kitchen, which is part of this area. I closed my eyes and tuned into the energies. I called in an earth dragon and asked it to clear the corner and the area behind the wall in my daughter's room. I called in Archangel Chamuel and asked him to place etheric mirrors to compensate for the missing space. I then walked into my daughter's room to get a feeling of the space there and smiled when I saw that she had photos displayed of herself and her boyfriend. Note: You should not activate areas for yourself in your children's rooms.

I did as much as I could to improve the situation, and the solution to activate my open heart area at a higher level involved doing it in a different room. My bedroom was not suitable due to a wardrobe in there, so it had to be the living room again. When I checked the area, I discovered that it is visually very pleasant and free from clutter. It falls halfway across the sofa, while behind is a huge image of the all-seeing eye of God. He watches over me, and I was very pleased when I discovered that this picture was in my open heart area, and it reminded me of my beautiful connection with Source. It is not where I usually sit to meditate but right next to it, and when I relax in the evening and lie down, I move into it. Interestingly, my son's place on the sofa falls into this area, so he gets bathed with love. But now, please read the information about Archangel Chamuel and then check out your Kun area, and let's clear it.

Meet Archangel Chamuel

Archangel Chamuel, the angel of love, appears with a beautiful pink-and-white aura. He radiates love and compassion. When you connect with his energy, your heart heals and opens, and you connect to the unconditional love in our universe. You feel loved and know the power of love. He can also add love to your home and any space. Archangel Chamuel is in charge of developing humanity's heart chakras at a fifth-dimensional level. He encourages all people to connect from heart to heart to bring about oneness. Archangel Chamuel's spiritual retreat is in St. Louis, Missouri, in the midwestern United States. His divine counterpart is Archangel Charity.

Tips on How to Interact with Archangels Chamuel and Charity

- Thinking of Archangel Chamuel or calling his name will draw his energy to you, and you can feel and attune to it.
- Ask Archangel Chamuel to fill you with his compassion, and allow yourself to feel nurtured.
- Feel Archangel Chamuel enfolding you in his immense wings, and see your heart centre radiate a magnificent pinkish-white light that flows into your body and aura.
- Ask Archangel Chamuel to fill your home with the highest love.
- You can say a prayer: "Beloved Archangel Chamuel, please help me see, act, and speak with love."
- Speak the affirmation: "I AM Archangel Chamuel."
  I AM affirmations are very powerful because they draw to you that which you are affirming. If you say "I AM Archangel Chamuel," your highest-dimensional aspect merges with Archangel Chamuel, and you draw his beautiful qualities to you.
- Ask Archangel Chamuel to fill all your relationships with love.
- Invoke Archangel Charity, and ask her to fill you with the divine quality of generosity.

VISUALIZATION to Clear the Kun Area

1. Sit in the space that represents the divine feminine in your home.
2. You may wish to light a candle and burn some incense. Clapping your hands will also clear the energies.
3. Set the intention to clear this area, raise the energy, and open your heart to higher love.
4. Call your angel of the home to supervise and hold the light. You can also call your guardian angel and your unicorn to come close.
5. Invoke an earth dragon and see it arrive. Its colour is brown like the earth, and like all dragons, it is very loving.
6. Ask the earth dragon to clear the space for you. Observe the earth dragon carrying out its task and blazing flames to clear the energies.
7. While the dragon is cleaning, reflect on whether you need to do anything else in this area. Should you remove or add things? You can have a conversation with the dragon and ask it for advice.
8. Ask the angel of the home to fill this space with light and add your love. Call in Archangel Chamuel, and ask him to add his light and love.
9. Thank the dragon, the angel of your home, and Archangel Chamuel.
10. Bring back your consciousness into your physical body, and open your eyes.

Personal Dragon Note

At this point in the book, I would like to connect you with your personal dragon, if you are not already working with your dragon to support your life path and help you transform. Just as you have a guardian angel and a personal unicorn, you can have a personal dragon to assist you on your journey who stays with you throughout your incarnation. Once you have established a connection with a dragon, it will remain for eternity and can work with you and guide you.

Dragons may appear fierce, but in reality, they are open-hearted and very loving. The dragon's wings are an extension of the love that radiates from their heart. I like comparing dragons to the spiritual warrior who is powerful but fights with deep love and wisdom.

My dragon encourages me to be a master of the heart. He shows me how to take three breaths and expand the energy of my heart further and further. Imagine throwing a stone into a pool and watching it ripple out into a big circle. A master of the heart is someone who acts, thinks, and sees with love, which is expected of everyone in the new Golden Age.

Your dragon makes a wonderful companion and friend. It will protect you if you ask. Like all higher beings, it respects your free will and cannot go against your freedom of choice or karma.

Dragons have a sense of humour. My dragon sometimes licks my face, and I think he does this just because he wants me to laugh and feel uplifted. Dragons have special magical abilities. They can change colour and size. I have always perceived my dragon as a blue-and-green energy, but recently, when I connected with him, I was surprised. When his energy came in, I felt incredibly moved. Then he shared a vision with me. I saw him looking completely different. Gone were his blue-and-green colours, and there he stood, immense and in a white aura of power on a high cliff, blazing white flames. It was an awe-inspiring vision.

I had a conversation with him.

"Wei, is that you?" I asked, almost shyly.

"Of course it's me," he responded with a huff.

"How come you look different?" I wanted to know.

"It is time for you to be more powerful!" he responded.

I understood. He came in at a more powerful and higher frequency because that was expected of me. He was showing me "the power of the dragon" that needs to be mastered. I gathered my courage and climbed onto his back, and he took off and flew down the steep mountain cliff at high speed. Eventually, we dived into the ocean. My dragon carries two elements, fire and water, so he loves gliding through the waves. That was okay, because I also love the water and shapeshifted into a mermaid to swim with him. I knew this experience signalled an important change in my life..

As you have probably already understood, dragons are elemental beings, and they do not have all four elements in their makeup. They can be composed of fire, earth, air, water, or a combination of up to three of them. Usually, your dragon is the same element as your astrological sign, so you automatically get a fire dragon if you are a fire sign. If you are a water sign, you may get a water dragon. However, there may be exceptions to this rule. If a fire dragon can support you best on your journey, one will come forward for you, even if you are a different sign. I am a fire sign, but my dragon's makeup is fire and water.

Your dragon works on a different frequency than your guardian angel and has different tasks, although the result is always the same: aligning you with your divine blueprint. Your dragon can physically clear lower energies around you and even manipulate matter, whereas your guardian angel focuses on the divine blueprint of your highest potential and will guide you towards manifesting it.

Note: I have referred to my own dragon as he, but you may, of course, perceive your dragon as a feminine energy.

What Can Your Dragon Do for You?

- Clear, low and dense energies around you.
- Support you with your spiritual development.
- Protect you—also when you travel in your spirit body.
- Open you up to higher energies.
- Clear your space and your ascension path.

Tips on How to Interact with Your Personal Dragon

- Establish a heart-to-heart connection by invoking your personal dragon every day. To call in my dragon by his name is part of my morning routine, like brushing my teeth.

I wouldn't feel right if I didn't call him. I just say his name and immediately feel his loving, protecting, and empowering energy around me.

- You can say the following prayer for protection and stepping into your power: "Beloved dragon, thank you for protecting me and lending me your power."
- You can ask your dragon to walk the highest path: "Beloved dragon, please clear my way with your blazing flames and raise my vibrations so I can walk the highest path."
- In the presence of your dragon, affirm three times: "I am powerful, and I walk with my dragon. Today, I can achieve anything. I have my dragon's full support." Repeating an affirmation three times increases its power.
- Compose a song to honour your dragon, and sing it. You will be amazed at how much that deepens your connection.

VISUALIZATION to Meet Your Personal Dragon and Receive Its Name

1. Close your eyes and relax.
2. Invoke golden-white Christ light into your space, and breathe it in. Focus on your breath. Breathe the light in and out into your aura. With each breath you take, you become more and more relaxed.
3. Call your dragon, and ask it to come close. Feel its loving presence and powerful energy. Observe your dragon. Does it have masculine or feminine energies? Look into its eyes and make a soul-to-soul connection. What colour are its eyes?
4. If this is the first time you have consciously connected with your dragon, you may wish to find out its name. Ask your dragon to drop its name into your mind now. Accept whatever name you are given, and trust it is the right vibration for connecting and working with your dragon.

5. Your dragon's job is to help you step into your power and become a master of the heart. Know that your dragon will stay close from now on and smooth your path for you. Thank your dragon for its support.

6. Feel your feet firmly on the ground, and open your eyes.

Meet the Goddess Kuan Yin

Kuan Yin is the Chinese Buddhist Goddess of Mercy and Compassion. Her energy is like the Tibetan Buddhist Tara energy, known for bringing release and comfort. Demonstrating the divine qualities of mercy, compassion, and forgiveness, she listens to every prayer or cry for help. She reaches out to you like a mother to her children when you are in need. Her energy is nurturing, soothes suffering, and is also very protective.

Kuan Yin had many lifetimes in China, and it is said that she had a 1,000-year incarnation. When she reached enlightenment, she decided to remain embodied because of her deep love of humanity. She also upheld the energy in the Temple of Love in Lemuria, a Golden Age that predates Atlantis.

Kuan Yin is in charge of the 12th ray of unconditional love that Source beams to Earth and is associated with a portal in the mountains of China that contains diamond-white love frequency. This portal will start to open as the frequencies of humanity rise, flood our Earth with the most beautiful pure love, and transform it to new levels we cannot imagine.

Below is a channelled message from Kuan Yin as a gift to facilitate your connection with her:

Beloved Reader,
See me reaching out to you right now. Feel my energy gently caressing you. Know that if you need me, I am there for you. Just call my name, and I will be right by your side to support you with my love and compassion.

Tips on How to Interact with Kuan Yin

- You can chant the sacred Sanskrit mantra *Om Mane Padme Hum* ("Hail to the Jewel in the Lotus") or *Om Tare Tuttare Ture Soha* (the Green Tara mantra) to raise your vibration above any fears and challenges. Years ago, when I was going through a really difficult time, I was given the *Om Tare Tuttare* mantra to chant daily, and it really helped me feel safe and looked after.

- Acquire a beautiful figurine of Kuan Yin. I have one on my altar to honour my connection with her and feel her presence in my home and her energy in my aura.

- You can ask Kuan Yin to look after your children and maintain harmony in your family.

- If you are facing a painful challenge call Kuan Yin, and she will enfold you with her gentle, nurturing energy and stay by your side until the issue is resolved.

- Kuan Yin would like me to share this short self-love visualization with you:

> *See yourself in a beautiful garden with Kuan Yin, admiring the pink blossoms of the trees. Kuan Yin asks you to stretch out your hand, and she puts a pink cherry petal into your hand. As soon as it touches your skin, a shower of cherry blossoms falls onto you, showering you with love and compassion. Kuan Yin embraces you, and you feel your heart overflow with love for yourself. Say out loud: "Beloved Kuan Yin, thank you for letting me know how much you love me."*

VISUALIZATION with Kuan Yin to Open Your Heart to Divine Feminine Love and Forgiveness

In this visualization, we will meet the goddess Kuan Yin in the Temple of Love to increase the flame of love in your heart, fill it with compassion and forgiveness, and heal your relationships. We will ask Kuan

Yin to connect the Kun area in your home with the ancient Temple of Love.

1. Sit in your Kun area, and close your eyes. Take a few deep breaths and relax.

2. With your mind's eye, see a mountain before you from which waterfalls are cascading. It is a truly magical sight.

3. Visualize yourself going up the winding mountain path, admiring the beautiful nature and the stunning views. Your personal dragon is by your side.

4. The path takes you near a waterfall. Step underneath, and take the opportunity to purify and refresh yourself. When you have finished, step back onto the path and continue climbing the mountain.

5. As you approach the top, you hear the bright and beautiful sound of wind chimes calling you. As you get closer, you see a temple shaped like a pagoda with an ethereal appearance and a pink glow. The wind chimes hanging by the entrance are made of crystal. They chime sacred notes as the wind blows through them, touching you deeply.

6. A priestess emerges and welcomes you warmly. Her appearance, too, is ethereal. You realize that your own body feels lighter. As you look down at yourself, you seem to glow with light. The priestess explains that you have reached the Temple of Love, which has existed since ancient times.

7. As you step into the temple, you see huge, clear crystals in different shapes lining the temple walls. In particular, you notice a huge twin-pointed crystal quartz. The priestess explains that they are Lemurian crystals and contain Source love. Stand before the twin-pointed crystal quartz, and let it bathe you with its loving energies, which transmit oneness and harmony.

8. The priestess is taking you to meet a special being. You find yourself standing before Kuan Yin, the Goddess of Compassion and Mercy. She wears a sparkling white dress with a pink cord

around her waist. Her black hair is piled up on her head, held with an exquisite golden coronet and decorated with flowers. Kuan Yin radiates pink light, and a small dragon sits on her shoulders. With awe, you bow to greet her. She smiles at you and raises her arms to embrace you. Being held within the arms of Kuan Yin is a most amazing feeling. She floods your heart with love and compassion, and her dragon looks at you curiously over her shoulder.

9. Kuan Yin knows that you have come here to open your heart to higher love. She leads you to an altar where a magnificent pink flame is burning within a golden urn. Dragons are guarding it. Kuan Yin explains that this is the flame of love. She invites you to gaze into the flame. She explains that the flame is also burning in the heart of Source, your heart, and everyone's heart. Contemplate the flame for as long as you want, intending to increase the flame of love in your heart.

10. Kuan Yin invites you into the temple garden for tea. As you walk through it, you notice the beautiful vibrant-coloured flowers and breathe in their scents. You take a seat. Kuan Yin pours the tea into a small delicate cup and offers it to you. You drink, and as the warm, fragrant liquid flows down your throat, it warms your heart. You are wondering what kind of tea this is, and Kuan Yin tells you it is the Tea of Compassionate Forgiveness.

11. Kuan Yin asks you whether you have any relationships that need healing. Think about it while you drink the tea. Let the images of people appear before your mind's eye. The tea's special ingredients help you open your heart to forgiveness. Take three deep breaths to expand the love in your heart and send it to those people. Visualize any energetic cords between you and these people dissolving and any freed spaces filling with love. You send out only loving and peaceful thoughts, with the knowledge that forgiveness brings joy into your heart and moves you onto a higher path.

12. You ask Kuan Yin to connect the Kun area in your home with her ancient Temple of Love. She nods her agreement, and the dragon on her shoulder spreads its wings and takes off. See it flying, and with a pink thread, it links the Temple of Love to your home. One of Kuan Yin's pink dragons will take on the task of guarding this link, making sure that love flows freely in the Kun area of your home.

13. It is time to return. Thank Kuan Yin for the grace that you have received. Rise and follow her through the garden and the temple exit. Together with your personal dragon, you descend the winding path. Take one more look at the beautiful mountain with cascading waterfalls, and bring your consciousness back into your space.

CONNECT with the Number Two

The number two brings divine feminine energy. With love and an open heart, you can achieve anything. It brings peace, creativity, caring, nurturing, togetherness, harmonious cooperation, and support. In a loving team, you can achieve more:

1. Close your eyes, and take a deep breath into your heart centre.
2. Visualize the turtle rising from the river water. You gaze at the two illuminated dots.
3. The turtle transports you to the ninth-dimensional pool of number two, right where it originates in the universe.
4. You dive into the pool, and heart-opening divine feminine energy streams into you.
5. You are absorbing the qualities of love, creativity, peace, caring, nurturing, and harmonious cooperation.
6. Thank the turtle for the loving energy it brought you and your home.

Intention for the Kun Area of Your Life

"I AM a master of the heart and radiate love always."

This is the intention and affirmation that dropped into my mind for the Kun area. You may wish to write your own, or you can use mine daily in the coming week.

ZHEN – The Gifts of the Ancestors

BAGUA AREA 3

This area of your bagua is called Zhen. The energy of the Zhen area is yin/yin/yang, and it is associated with the eldest son—the energy being enthusiastic, confident, assertive, and focused.

Zhen symbolizes thunder, and its element is wood. Zhen traditionally represents your family, and the keywords for this area are ancestors, heritage, legacy, and foundation. For our purposes on my 5D Bagua of Higher Aspirations, I have called it The Gifts of the Ancestors, because we want to focus on the highest perspective.

I have given this bagua area the colour silver. I felt silver is the perfect colour to create a solid foundation. It is associated with the Earth Star chakra below your feet, which anchors you deep into the earth, and Archangel Sandalphon, who is in charge of developing that centre at a fifth-dimensional level for humanity.

Who were your ancestors? What are your roots? Have you ever considered these questions? How do you feel about your ancestors? Are your thoughts about them loving, not so kind, or neutral? Or maybe you never thought about them. Take some time for research. Try to find out the names of your grandparents, great-grandparents, great-great-grandparents, and so on, from your older relatives.

No matter what you think about your ancestors, they have gifts for you. Being aware of this and acknowledging it makes their lives worthwhile. You can also pray for them to reach the next level of their evolution. Knowing your ancestors and clearing family karma can help you fortify your foundations and move forward with confidence in your life.

I am discovering, in this instant, that the Zhen area covers half of my living room, which is my highest-frequency space. Also, applying the whole bagua to this one room, the white table where I am being creative, producing my work, falls exactly on the Zhen square. I have a permanent altar and crystals on my table, and every morning, I light a candle and burn incense. It feels perfect. Now check where your Zhen area is, and let's clear it.

VISUALIZATION to Clear the Zhen Area

1. Sit in the space that represents the Zhen area in your home.
2. You may wish to light a candle and burn some incense.
3. Close your eyes and relax.
4. Set the intention to clear this area, raise the energy, and create a solid foundation for your life at a higher level.
5. Call the angel of your home to supervise and hold the light. You can also call your guardian angel and your personal unicorn to come close.
6. Once more, invoke an earth dragon. Imagine that the space you are sitting in becomes a magical wood containing majestic trees with strong roots. As you breathe in, you can smell their scent.
7. Ask the earth dragon to clear the space for you. Observe it, moving from tree to tree, carrying out its task and blazing flames to clear the energies.
8. While the dragon is clearing, reflect on whether there is anything else to be done in this area. Should you remove or add things? You can have a conversation with the dragon, the angel of your home, or your unicorn, and ask them for advice.
9. Ask the angel of your home to fill this space with light, and add your love and gratitude.
10. Thank the earth dragon, your unicorn, and the angel of your home for the cleansing and insights.
11. Come back with your consciousness into your physical body, and open your eyes.

Your Immediate Ancestors

The next step for this area is to invoke your immediate ancestors, going back seven generations to clear any ancestral karma, honour these forebears, and receive and appreciate all the gifts they bring. Your immediate ancestors are your parents, grandparents, great-grandparents, great-great-grandparents, and so on. Those who are alive will join you in their spirit body. We will invoke the Lords of Karma to assist us in this work, so please first read the information below on karma, the karmic board, and how to write the petition.

Karma Note

Karma is the Law of Cause and Effect. Everything you do, say, or think has an effect, and this is how you create your own reality. According to Diana Cooper, there was a huge influx of crystalline diamond energy in 2015, with the result that all we do, say, or think on this planet will come back as instant karma. This means the effect will be visible immediately, whereas it may have taken lifetimes in the past. I have noticed that if I do something in the morning that is not aligned with my usual way of being, I will notice the effect in the afternoon and can work at dissolving it.

There are different types of karma: personal, ancestral, and the karma of a town, country, or planet. We will focus on your personal and ancestral karma in the next visualization. With the shift of energies on Earth, we are asked to dissolve all karma and are given special dispensations to do so quickly. Once you have made the best efforts to learn and understand your lesson, you can petition the 12 Lords of Karma to free you from karma or its impact.

The 12 Lords of Karma

The Lords of Karma are mighty beings with the role of overseeing and balancing all types of karma.

The karmic board members, as given by Diana Cooper are:

- **The Great Divine Director** – a being very close to Source

- **The Goddess of Liberty** – Charity in Atlantis and Libertas in Roman mythology
- **Lady Nada** – the twin flame of Sananda
- **Pallas Athena** – Goddess of Truth and Wisdom
- **Elohim Vista** – a Creator angel
- **Kuan Yin** – Goddess of Mercy and Compassion
- **Lady Portia** – Goddess of Justice and Opportunity
- **Jesus** – bringer of Cosmic Love
- **Josiah** – a master from Sirius who helps souls transition during earthquakes and volcano eruptions
- **Abraham** – an aspect of the Ascended Master El Morya
- **Peter the Great** – in charge of environmental movements and helping shift humanity's consciousness towards animals
- **Catherine of Siena** – in charge of activating the spiritual light within every person.

How to Interact with the Lords of Karma

- Interact with the Lords of Karma with great respect.
- Invoke them by saying each name out loud, or connect with a particular one that you feel attracted to.
- Petition the Lords of Karma when you feel that you have tried your best to resolve a particular situation.

Write a Petition to the Lords of Karma

Before doing the visualization, I invite you to draft a petition addressed to the Lords of Karma. Do this with humility, reverence, pure intentions, and under the Law of Grace. Grace pours from the heart of Source. It is a divine mercy that dissolves all lower vibrations. It replaces the old with a new pure light and sets everyone free.

Be willing to accept and understand the lessons and opportunities for growth your family karma has brought you—in your heart, there should only be love, compassion, and forgiveness. Be open to receiving and giving grace.

Remember, your ancestors were defined by the circumstances into which they were born and by their own parents. I have included your parents in this first visualization, but we will also work with them more intensively in the next step. Before doing the visualization, you may wish to create a sacred space. Set up a little altar with a candle and amethyst crystal if you have them, or anything else you want to add; the amethyst crystal is perfect for releasing and transmuting old energies.

Here is an example of a petition:

Beloved Lords of Karma,
Under grace and with pure intention, I petition you to clear the
effects of any ancestral karma for me and the seven generations
of family gathered here. I accept all lessons and vow to grow
spiritually as much as I possibly can. I am dedicated to serving
Source, humanity, and the Universe to the best of my ability.

VISUALIZATION to Honour Your Immediate Ancestors

1. Close your eyes and relax.
2. Focus on your breath. With each breath, relax more and more. As you breathe in and out, relax your body and mind.
3. Invoke Archangel Michael, the angel of protection, courage, and strength, to oversee your work and act as a gatekeeper.
4. Call your guardian angel and dragon to come close.
5. Focus on your heart. Watch your dragon take three deep breaths, and do the same to expand your heart energy. See and feel the love in your heart rippling outwards in a sphere. Repeat the affirmation: "I AM a master of the heart."
6. Invoke your parents. Visualize Archangel Michael opening a portal of light. See your parents stepping through the portal accompanied by angels. Bow to your parents, and bless them. Send them love from your heart, and thank them for their gifts. Focus on them for as long as you wish.

7. Invoke your grandparents from both your mother's side and your father's side. Visualize them stepping through the portal accompanied by angels. Bow to your grandparents, and bless all four of them. Send them love from your heart, and thank them for their gifts.

8. Invoke your great-grandparents from both your mother's side and your father's side. Visualize them stepping through the portal accompanied by angels. Bow to your great-grandparents, and bless all eight of them. Send them love from your heart and thank them for their gifts.

9. Invoke your great-great-grandparents from both your mother's side and your father's side. Visualize them stepping through the portal accompanied by angels. Bow to your great-great-grandparents, and bless all 16 of them. Send them love from your heart, and thank them for their gifts.

10. Invoke your great-great-great-grandparents from both your mother's side and your father's side. Visualize them stepping through the portal accompanied by angels. Bow to your great-great-great-grandparents, and bless all 32 of them. Send them love from your heart, and thank them for their gifts.

11. Invoke your great-great-great-great-grandparents from both your mother's side and your father's side. Visualize them stepping through the portal accompanied by angels. Bow to your great-great-great-great-grandparents, and bless all 64 of them. Send them love from your heart and thank them for their gifts.

12. Invoke your great-great-great-great-great-grandparents from both your mother's side and your father's side. Visualize them stepping through the portal accompanied by angels. Bow to your great-great-great-great-great-grandparents, and bless all 108 of them. Send them love from your heart, and thank them for their gifts.

13. You have 234 ancestors gathered now, bringing you gifts. Feel gratitude in your heart, and reflect on what these gifts might be. Each person has different qualities, skills, knowledge, experiences, and wisdom. Remember that all beings incarnating on Earth are courageous, high-frequency souls with much to share from their many lifetimes on Earth, other planets and stars, and even other universes. Your ancestors may offer you strength, love, and compassion, or they can help you anchor more deeply into the planet.

14. Invoke the Lords of Karma, and sense them joining you. Bow to greet them. Read your petition for the effects of any ancestral karma and family karma to be cleared for you and all your family, reaching back seven generations. Stay in silence, and receive the response from the Lords of Karma. Thank them, and watch them retreat.

15. As you look at your ancestors again, the angels are flooding them with light. You may see illuminated symbols in their auras and recognize that they are truly magnificent souls. You may feel love and gratitude coming towards you. Once more, bow to your ancestors to honour them, and thank them for coming. Tell them you are very thankful for their gifts and the grace you have received.

16. It is time for them to return. Watch your ancestors and their angels step through the portal that Archangel Michael keeps open for them. When the last one has gone, he closes it. Start bringing your consciousness back into your physical body. Know that something has shifted. Your foundations are stronger, and this is a new beginning. Open your eyes and expect wondrous things to happen.

Your Parents

Next, we will work with your parents. Your parents can affect your whole life, even when you are an adult and they have passed over.

No one has perfect parents. Before we incarnate, we make soul contracts. Your parents will have agreed to have you as a child. That is an act of service to be honoured. You will have chosen the perfect parents for the lessons you have come to learn.

For example, if your parents were manipulative, your lesson may be to act with integrity, or if your parents were critical, your lesson may be to approve of yourself and know that you are a divine being. Your parents were defined by the circumstances into which they were born and by their own parents. Try to find out about your parents' childhood to help understand them. They have probably brought you up to the best of their ability, allowing you to learn your chosen lessons.

VISUALIZATION to Meet Your Parents in Their Spirit Body

1. Close your eyes and relax.
2. Visualize yourself sitting in the shade of a majestic tree with your personal dragon. The sun is shining, and the wind is blowing through the branches.
3. Send your roots deep into the earth. Intertwining your roots with those of the tree allows you to ground yourself.
4. Your dragon invites you to open your heart. It shows you how by taking three deep breaths and making its heart glow in its chest. You do the same. Let your heart expand beyond your throat chakra and your solar plexus.
5. The tree you are sitting under is special. It is an ancient guardian tree with incredible wisdom to share. It is tall and has withstood many storms. Take some time to talk with the tree about your parents, and while you do so, maintain your open heart. The tree may have some wisdom to share with you about your parents, so listen to what it has to say.
6. Suddenly, the wind increases. You hear thunder cracking, and as you look up into the sky, you see lightning flashing. Clouds have gathered, and rain starts falling. You are safe

and sheltered under the tree and supported by its powerful aura. You are aware of the power of thunder to clear lower energies and that rain is cleansing.

7. You see a figure coming towards the tree. It is your mother. She is in her body of light and wears a flowing robe. You are seeing her from a soul level. You call out to her to join you under the tree. She smiles when she sees you and approaches quickly.

8. From soul to soul, send your mother love. Thank her for agreeing to give birth to you and allowing you to incarnate on Earth during these exciting times. Tell her that you know she has brought you up to the best of her abilities and that you can now take care of yourself. You have some time to talk to your mother with love, compassion, grace, and forgiveness in your heart. Thank her for all you have learnt.

9. Your mother is very grateful for the talk and leaves. She is in her spirit body, so the thunder and rain won't affect her.

10. You see another figure coming towards the tree. It is your father. He, too, is in his body of light and wears a flowing robe. Invite him to join you under the tree. Thank him for bringing you up to the best of his abilities, and tell him that you can now take care of yourself. Take time to talk to your father with love, compassion, grace, and forgiveness in your heart.

11. Your father is very grateful for the talk and leaves. Watch him walk away through the trees, and when you no longer see him, the thunderstorm stops.

12. Thank the tree for its support and wisdom and for sheltering you. Slowly return with your consciousness into the space where you started and fully into your physical body. Open your eyes, take a deep breath, and focus on the love in your heart.

Cosmic Parents for the New Golden Age

I want to take the concept of "ancestors" further. In ancient times, there were highly evolved civilizations, such as the Lemurians, Atlanteans, Egyptians, Babylonians, Maya, and so on. You probably know that you have had Atlantean or Lemurian lives, and therefore, Atlantean or Lemurian parents. You may have had parents on other stars and planets. These are your more distant ancestors, and they, too, have gifts for you. This is particularly important as we have to bring back this ancient wisdom and these ancient energies in order for Earth to shift into the new Golden Age.

Acknowledging your lineage gives you a solid foundation in your current incarnation. It helps you understand who you are.

The following visualization aims to connect you with the parents who vibrate at the perfect frequency for the new Golden Age. You can call them your Cosmic Parents.

VISUALIZATION to Meet Your Cosmic Parents
(Note: If possible, hold a crystal while you perform this visualization.)
1. Close your eyes and relax.
2. Once more, visualize yourself sitting in the shade of the ancient guardian tree with your personal dragon. It is a peaceful day, and a breeze blows through the branches.
3. The tree's big and strong roots remind you to send your own roots deep into the earth in order to ground yourself. As you do so, intertwine your roots with the tree roots.
4. Your guardian tree is now talking to you about your distant lineage. It reminds you that throughout your incarnations, you had many different parents, some highly evolved from different eras, planes of existence, or other planets. You can call them your Cosmic Parents, because they are not part of the earthly realm now. Your guardian

tree suggests that you meet with your Cosmic Mother and Cosmic Father. They have the perfect gifts to share with you to guide you into the new Golden Age.

5. Your dragon will accompany you on this journey. Follow it along a path through the trees. The birds are singing their messages, and you breathe in the fresh fragrant scents from the surrounding nature. Your dragon leads you to a bridge. You can see a clear stream flowing over rocks as you look down. Your dragon invites you to cross the bridge. Step onto it, and cross it in 11 steps. You see a beautiful angel waiting for you as you approach the other side.

6. The angel greets you warmly and tells you that they will take you to meet your Cosmic Mother. Follow the angel along a golden path, and take a look around. Do you see any particular landmarks? Where are you? Are there houses or temples, or are you in nature? Are there any bodies of water? Do you see people? You can ask the angel to give you information about where you are.

7. The angel is taking you to the perfect place to meet your Cosmic Mother. You have reached it now. What is it? A house, a temple, a garden, or somewhere else?

8. Whatever it is, you have reached your destination. You are now gazing at your Cosmic Mother. Your connection with her goes beyond time and space. Take some time to observe her clothing, hair, and expression. Her face is beaming with joy to see you. But what strikes you most is the powerful love she radiates towards you.

9. Your Cosmic Mother now steps forward and takes your hands. She emanates divine feminine energies. Her heart is glowing with compassion and love for you. She is here to share her wisdom and nurture you. You have some time to communicate with her. Ask her about the life you had together, and listen to any advice she may have for you.

10. Your Cosmic Mother now shares a gift with you. Take time to understand the gift and how she shares it. Thank your Cosmic Mother, and take your leave.

11. The angel will take you now to meet your Cosmic Father. Follow the angel once more along the golden path. The scenery may change completely. Take time to observe and work out where you are. You can ask the angel.

12. You have reached your destination. You are now gazing at your Cosmic Father. Your connection with him goes beyond time and space. Take some time to observe his clothing, hair, and expression. He smiles, and his benevolent eyes sparkle with joy to see you.

13. Your Cosmic Father now steps forward and takes your hands. He emanates divine masculine energies; in particular, strength and protection. He is here to encourage and support you in all your endeavours. You have some time to communicate with him. Listen to what he has to say.

14. Your Cosmic Father now shares his gift with you. Take time to understand what it is and how he shares it. Thank your Cosmic Father, and take your leave.

15. Follow the angel back along the golden path. As you walk together, the angel tells you that your Cosmic Parents are here to support you with your next evolutionary step into the new Golden Age. With them, you can achieve anything. Know that you can invoke them just by thinking of them.

16. You have reached the bridge now and, together with your dragon, take 11 steps to reach the other side. Return along the path to your guardian tree. It looks at you knowingly and blesses your path once more.

17. Bring your consciousness back into your space, and bring your new gifts with you.

CONNECT with the Number Three

Number three is about reaching up and connecting with the higher realms while anchoring firmly into the earth, like a tree. It allows higher inspiration to flow into you and creativity to emerge. It helps you to inspire others and transmit happiness. It brings relaxation, optimism, enthusiasm, motivation, and the ability to communicate and express yourself.

1. Close your eyes, and take a deep breath.
2. Visualize the turtle rising from the flowing river water. Three dots are glowing on its back.
3. The turtle invites you on a journey to the cosmic pool of number three.
4. Higher inspiration flows into you as you bathe in the energy of number three with the turtle.
5. You are receiving the qualities of relaxation, happiness, optimism, enthusiasm, and motivation for moving forward.
6. You are also receiving the ability to communicate and express yourself, ground yourself, and reach the higher realms with your consciousness.
7. Thank the turtle for the inspiration and happiness it brought you and return safely to your own space..

Intention for the Zhen Area of Your Life

> *"I am deeply grounded into the earth and confidently move forward into the new Golden Age."*

Please repeat this affirmation for the coming week, or write your own for the Zhen area.

XUN – Open Up to Abundance

BAGUA AREA 4

This his area of your bagua is called Xun. The energy of the Xun area is yang/yang/yin, and it is associated with the energy of the eldest daughter: persistent, sensitive, positive, creative, communicative, and harmonious. Xun symbolizes wind, and its element is wood. Xun traditionally represents wealth. On my 5D Bagua of Higher Aspirations, I have called it Open Up to Abundance.

I have given this bagua area the colour emerald green. I felt that emerald green is the perfect colour, because it is associated with the light of Archangel Raphael, the angel of healing and abundance.

Xun is about the flow of prosperity, abundance, and gratitude in your life. It is about opening up to receive and give in a balanced way, and gratitude is a key to abundance if you really feel it in the heart. When your abundance codes are activated, prosperity, love, success, blessings, peace, and any other divine quality you wish for will flow towards you. This is your divine right, and how it should be. We live in an abundant universe with infinite riches to share, and all these qualities are available to you.

I have discovered that the Xun area covers half my living room, my highest-frequency space. Also, applying the whole bagua to this one room, the Xun area falls on what I call my "indoor garden." I have a corner in my living room with vibrant green plants, including money plants. Living things bring more energy into the home, and plants also render the air fresher.

I have placed some stones and a beautiful citrine crystal here. Citrine brings abundance.

On the wall is a Flower of Life decoration that purifies the energies. I placed it there as it is where the wifi is located. The Flower of Life symbol is about the interconnectedness of everything and has the power to raise frequencies. Within the Xun area is an altar and my vision board. I create a vision board of what I want to manifest at the beginning of the year, and intuitively, I had placed it in the perfect spot.

Now check where your Xun area is. Decide whether to activate it where it falls on your complete floor plan, in a particular room, or both. In my home, the two areas overlap. But now, please read the information about the air dragons and Archangel Raphael, and let's clear the Xun area.

Air Dragon Note

As the name suggests, air dragons are connected with the element of air. They love flying and are aligned with the wind. They are fourth-dimensional beings and are blue like the sky. They carry the qualities of lightness, soaring in the skies, and hope, and they can greatly inspire you. Air dragons are specially qualified to blow away dense energies and anything old that no longer serves you, including beliefs and limiting thoughts. They can use the wind to blow in new high-frequency ideas and inspirations that move you forward on your path. They can help you speak your truth openly and lovingly.

Tips on How to Interact with an Air Dragon

- Befriend the air dragons in your area. Go outside into nature, and simply call to the air dragons and greet them. You can ask them for a sign that they have heard you. You may hear the rustling of leaves.
- If you have a repeating limiting thought or belief, say: "Beloved air dragon, please remove this thought from my mind and replace it with a higher positive one." Sit still, allow the dragon to carry out this task, then ask it to drop a new high-frequency thought into your mind.

- Ask an air dragon to sweep through a space to clear any dense energies.
- If you want to be more creative, go outside on a windy day and say, "Beloved air dragon, please help me awaken my creativity and have inspiring ideas."
- Remember to be always grateful and thank the air dragon.

Meet Archangel Raphael

Archangel Raphael is the angel of healing, abundance, and vision. He appears with a glorious emerald-green light, and is in charge of developing the third-eye chakra for all of humanity at a fifth-dimensional level. He can clear your third eye and free you from illusions. When you connect with his energy, you can experience healing in all your bodies.

Archangel Raphael can help you with enlightenment and see and manifest from the higher perspective of love. He can also help you see how magnificent and divine you are. Archangel Raphael helps you open yourself to abundance consciousness and accept cosmic abundance into your life. His spiritual retreat is in Fatima, Portugal. Archangel Raphael's twin flame is Archangel Mary, who has her retreat in Lourdes.

Tips on How to Interact with Archangel Raphael

- Connect with Archangel Raphael by thinking or saying his name and visualizing his beautiful, healing emerald light all around you.
- You can ask Archangel Raphael and his emerald-green dragons to fly over the world and bring healing to those in need.
- You can say the following prayer for someone who is ill: "Beloved Archangel Raphael, under grace, I pray for the healing and highest good of (add name). So be it." Visualize Archangel Raphael holding that person's hand and accompanying them towards recovery.

- Ask Archangel Raphael for a download of the keys and codes of abundance.
- Say the affirmation "I AM Archangel Raphael" to draw his beautiful light and qualities to you.
- You can ask your spirit to visit Archangel Raphael's spiritual retreat at night when you sleep to receive healing.
- Call upon Archangel Raphael to clear your third eye and remove the veils of illusion so you can see only love and truth.
- If you have an emerald, you can use it to connect with Archangel Raphael. The emerald is Archangel Raphael's energy solidified.

VISUALIZATION to Clear the Xun Area

1. Sit in the space that represents the Xun area in your home.
2. You may wish to light a candle and burn some incense.
3. Close your eyes and relax. Take a few deep breaths into your heart.
4. Set the intention to clear this area, raise the energy, and increase the flow of abundance in your life.
5. Call the angel of your home to supervise and hold the light. You can also call your guardian angel and your personal unicorn and dragon to come close.
6. Imagine that the space you are sitting in becomes a small wood, and a clear stream flows through it. You are looking upon beautiful, magical trees with strong roots nurturing themselves with the water. The wind is blowing through the branches. Fresh air enters your lungs as you breathe in, and the tree scent is reinvigorating.
7. See a beautiful water dragon emerge from the stream and ask it to clear your Xun area with water and love. As you look up into the air, you see an air dragon flying above the trees. Ask it to help clear the area, too. See it blowing air to clear the area with the help of the wind.

8. While the dragons are clearing, reflect on whether there is anything else to be done in this area. Should you remove or add things? You can talk with the dragons and the angel of your home and ask them for advice.

9. Ask the angel of your home to fill this space with light, and add your love.

10. Invoke Archangel Raphael, and ask him to bless this area and add his emerald light containing the keys and codes of abundance.

11. Thank the dragons and the angel of your home for the cleansing and insights.

12. Come back with your consciousness into your physical body, and open your eyes.

Reflections on My Xun Area

My usual meditation spot falls into this area, and I sat with this visualization for a very long time. Observing my space, I had many wonderful revelations. My heart was overflowing with gratitude for the plants and the crystals continuously keeping the frequencies high. It is good to have images of water or waterfalls in this area, because water nurtures wood and brings vitality and health, so I included it in the clearing visualization.

I don't have any water images, but I had the intuition to take the concept to a higher level. I asked Dora, the angel of my home, and the dragons to anchor this flowing stream and trees at an etheric level in this space. I named it the Stream of Everflowing Abundance, and it flows into an imaginary ocean beyond my home. I also imagined water elementals in the stream, particularly undines, singing and clearing it. They have an ethereal presence and shimmering auras. Water carries the energy of cosmic love, and the undines and the water dragons keep the love flowing.

My living room has come alive with wondrous things, and I now see it completely differently. On a practical level, I was also told not to keep my work folders on the floor, so I put them inside a cupboard. Another suggestion was adding a shell to this area, which I am doing right now. And I added an image of the Goddess of the Oceans.

I am now observing what is behind my living room wall with my mind's eye, because my Xun area also covers a strip of my bedroom, where the head of my bed is. A beautiful blue wall decoration depicts the Goddess of the Oceans with fish and stars. She represents the flow of abundance. So again, I am amazed that I had intuitively placed her in the perfect spot. Close to the window, there are also dolphin wind chimes in this area that keep the energy flowing.

Activating Your Abundance Codes

When the abundance codes are activated, your thinking and feeling align, and you experience an increase in faith, self-love, worthiness, deservingness, and manifestation power. Do you need to change your mindset? Believe that you are a master manifester and can reach all your goals. What you focus on manifests, and it is very important to set yourself goals. I do this at the beginning of each month and also on the new moon. Higher visions will bring you onto a higher path, and you should expect amazing opportunities to present themselves. When they do, you are called to action. It is "action" that brings changes into your life. Time does not exist in the higher dimensions, so it is possible to call in the aspect of yourself already living your abundant dream life to merge with you and guide you.

The 12-Chakra System, according to Diana Cooper

In the next visualization, we will activate your abundance codes, and I have nominated the 12 chakras from Diana Cooper's system. As you may not be familiar with them, I would like to explain them first. Most importantly, you will note that the fifth-dimensional chakra colours differ from the third-dimensional ones. It is important to start working with the new colours to advance on your ascension path. As you raise your frequency, you may see different colours. Trust and accept, if that happens. There are also specific archangels associated with each chakra who are in charge of developing them at the fifth dimension for all of humanity.

What are chakras? Chakras are vortices of energy in the body that react in relation to your emotions, thoughts, and experiences. You can imagine them opening like flowers as they activate. Healthy and clear chakras spin in rhythm with each other. Each chakra has a number of chambers associated with the lessons you are learning in this lifetime, or you may have mastered them already in your past incarnations. The chakras are interconnecting wheels, so they must all be open and balanced to work effortlessly together and allow light to flow through all your systems. Incredible wisdom flows through each of them, and when you work with your chakras, you can consciously access that knowledge.

At the time of Golden Atlantis, a 1500-year period during which the energies were high and pure, all people were fifth-dimensional. They had 12 active chakras, bringing them extraordinary psychic gifts and powers. When this Golden Age ended, the frequency on Earth dropped, and it became a third-dimensional world. As a result, five fifth-dimensional chakras were closed down and left humanity with the seven chakras that many people are familiar with. With the planet's rising energies, we are asked to activate the dormant chakras in the fifth dimension and access their qualities and gifts. This is essential for both your individual and the collective ascension of humanity and the planet. In the golden future, the whole of humanity will be fifth-dimensional again.

The **Earth Star chakra** is a silver chakra below your feet. Here, you hold your divine potential for this lifetime. As you evolve, the chakra expands, and at the same time, your potential and golden opportunities grow, allowing you to align with your life purpose. The Earth Star is your connection to Mother Earth and anchors you deep into the planet. This is incredibly important, because you need to be deeply grounded to work with higher energies. The Earth Star is the centre of your spiritual foundation and contains your fifth-dimensional divine blueprint. Archangel Sandalphon looks after this chakra.

The **base chakra** is a beautiful, shining platinum light located at the base of your spine. This centre holds your sense of security. When it is open and activated at a fifth-dimensional level, you know that the Universe will readily provide you with all you need and more. You feel safe, secure, balanced, and looked after. You have total trust in Source to sustain you for your highest good. Archangel Gabriel is in charge of this centre.

The **sacral chakra** is delicate pink and located in the lower abdomen. This centre is about your relationships, forgiveness, and embracing higher sexuality. When you activate this chakra at the fifth-dimensional level, you express transcendent love. You can be yourself, shine your magnificent light, experience pure love, and attract loving and respectful relationships. Archangel Gabriel also looks after the sacral chakra.

The **navel chakra** is vibrant orange and located at the navel. This centre, when activated in the fifth dimension, allows you to embrace the divine in all beings. You radiate welcoming, warm energy and cooperate with everyone for the highest good. It is this centre that allows Oneness consciousness to return to Earth. Archangel Gabriel is in charge of the navel chakra.

The **solar plexus chakra** is gold and holds your personal power, self-worth, and self-confidence. It is the seat of your gut feelings, and your higher self uses it to bring your awareness to the changes you need to make. When fully fifth-dimensional, it radiates golden wisdom, and you feel deep inner peace. It allows you to see the good in people and be a master of your energies. Archangel Uriel is in charge of this centre.

The **heart chakra** is pure white. Here, you develop unconditional love, compassion, and empathy for all there is. When you activate this centre at the fifth-dimensional level, you can connect directly to the divine love of Source through the Cosmic Heart (the planet Venus, the heart chakra of our universe). You can achieve this by seeing with the eyes of love and recognize that every person is a part of Source and has a divine spark residing in them. Archangel Chamuel is in charge of the heart chakra.

The **throat chakra** is royal blue, and through this centre, you express your truth. When you activate the throat chakra at the fifth-dimensional level, your words become sacred, you speak with integrity, and you co-create with Source. You master higher communication skills. At the same time, your aura becomes pure and radiates the light of integrity, honesty, and authenticity. Archangel Michael looks after this centre for humanity.

The **third-eye chakra** is crystal clear, and at the upper level of the fifth dimension, it glows with emerald light. It is the centre of clairvoyance, and here, you develop your inner vision and wisdom. When it activates at the fifth-dimensional level, the veils of illusion dissolve, and you become all-knowing and all-seeing. You reclaim your spiritual gifts and can then use your third eye to see all that you need to know, whether in the past, present, or future. Archangel Raphael is in charge of the third eye.

The **crown chakra** is also crystal clear and glows with golden light at the upper level of the fifth dimension. Here, you accept the light of your soul and connect to stars, planets, and galaxies. The crown chakra is likened to the 1,000-petalled lotus because it has 1,000 chambers, each of which can connect you to the wisdom of a star or planet. You surrender to the higher consciousness of Source, the angels, and the masters, and accept that you are part of a divine plan and have a mission to fulfil. Archangel Jophiel looks after this centre.

The **causal chakra** is pure white and located behind the centre of the back of the head when it first activates at the fourth dimension. As you evolve into the fifth dimension, it moves above the crown into alignment with the other chakras. The causal chakra radiates purity and eternal peace. It is your gateway to the angelic realms. When you activate it at the fifth-dimensional level, it facilitates your communication with angels, unicorns, and other higher beings and allows you to receive divine inspiration. It also allows unicorns to use it as a portal to come to Earth. Archangel Christiel looks after this centre.

The **Soul Star chakra** is a vibrant magenta colour located approximately 50 centimetres above the top of your head and activates in the fifth dimension. Your soul is on a journey. You may have had many incarnations on Earth, other star systems, and other universes. All your soul lessons and wisdom are recorded in this chakra. As you go through the lessons, you gain soul wisdom and mastery. Archangels Zadkiel and Mariel look after this centre.

The **Stellar Gateway chakra** is located about 1 meter above your head, and its colour is gold. This chakra vibrates in the sixth dimension, allowing you access to Source energy. When you have mastered the divine qualities in this centre, you can merge with your highest-dimensional aspect, the Monad, which is the original divine spark created by Source. The archangel developing this centre for humanity is glorious Archangel Metatron.

VISUALIZATION to Activate Your Abundance Codes

1. Sit in the space that represents the Xun area in your home.
2. Close your eyes and relax.
3. Call your angel of the home, your guardian angel, and your personal unicorn and dragon to come close. We are also calling in Source to assist and Archangel Raphael to overlight.
4. See your Xun area as a small wood with a wide, clear stream flowing through it. You can hear the sound of the flowing water, and as you breathe in, you feel refreshed.
5. Take three deep breaths into your heart, and feel this centre expand. Connect with your heart, and think about what kind of life you want to lead in a year from now. Take a few minutes for this.
6. Now enter the stream. The clear water carries love and is the perfect temperature, refreshing and healing.

Your friend, the water dragon, emerges from below and joins you, emanating a golden light and spreading love as it moves through the current. Take some time to greet and connect with it.

7. Set the intention to release any limitations so you can enjoy the abundance you deserve. Ask the water dragon to use its loving energy to dissolve any limiting beliefs, patterns, and thoughtforms in your energy fields so your aura can expand. The larger your aura is, the more abundance can flow into it.

8. We start with the 12 chakras. The dragon breathes into your heart chakra. Its love is so powerful that you feel your heart centre expand. Next, it breathes into your solar plexus, navel, sacral, base, and Earth Star chakras. Then it breathes into your throat, third eye, crown, causal chakra, Soul Star, and Stellar Gateway chakras. See your chakras becoming one unified column. This column extends deep into the earth and high up into the heavens and the heart of Source.

9. The water dragon breathes love and light into your physical and etheric body. It breathes into your emotional and mental body to clear them. Your sentiments are lofty, and your thoughts are high-frequency and noble. They are the thoughts of a master determined to move forward on their path. Next, the water dragon breathes into your spiritual bodies all the way up through the dimensions. See your aura sparkling with high-frequency light and colours, and see it expanding beyond your home, city, country, world, galaxy, and universe.

10. Suddenly, you feel lifted out of the water. As you look down, you notice that you are on the back of a huge turtle, and its shell is illuminated with golden symbols. The water dragon chuckles as it sees the surprise on your face. The dragon explains that they are abundance codes written in

light language. "Do you want to receive these abundance keys?" it asks you. You nod, and watch them flow from the turtle's back into your energy fields.

11. Your aura spans the universe, and your chakras connect with the stars. Your aura is a vessel and container for the infinite abundance of the Universe, and you see and feel it flowing into your fields from the heart of Source. Take a deep breath, and stand in your power on the turtle's back. Feel an increase in faith, trust, self-worth, self-love, deservingness, gratitude, and manifestation power as the keys and codes take up their rightful place in your aura.

12. Once more, visualize the life you want to lead in a year's time and invoke the aspect of yourself that is already living it to merge with you and share its secrets. Become one, and fill your heart with immense gratitude.

13. The water dragon has a gift for you. It shows you a shimmering pearl in its claw. Hold out your hand to accept the pearl. "This pearl symbolizes abundance and infinite opportunities," the dragon tells you. "It is yours now."

14. Thank the water dragon, turtle, and Source for what you have received. The turtle descends into the waters, and you make your way to the stream bank, where your guardian angel, unicorn, and dragon await you with big smiles on their faces. They know you have made a huge shift.

15. Bring your consciousness back into your physical body. Open your eyes, knowing that you always have access to the infinite abundance of the Universe. You are a master manifester and can reach all your goals.

CONNECT with the Number Four

Number four is about stability and security. Its influence helps you build a solid foundation for your life, your mission, and the flow of the abundance you deserve.

1. Close your eyes, and take a deep breath.
2. Visualize the turtle rising from the clear water of the Luo River, and with fascination, you observe the map on its back. The four dots are glowing brightly and magically.
3. The turtle invites you onto its back and flies you right into the cosmic pool of number four.
4. You are bathing in the qualities for creating a solid foundation for your life, your mission, and the flow of abundance you deserve.
5. The energy of practicality and dependability is streaming into you. You are receiving the ability to be orderly and systematic.
6. The turtle in the water with you radiates keys and codes of abundance and prosperity towards you.
7. Thank the turtle for the abundance it brought you, and return with your consciousness back to your space.

Intention for the Xun Area of Your Life

> *"My aura spans the Universe, and infinite abundance is flowing through me."*

Please repeat this affirmation for the coming week, or write your own for the Xun area.

TAIJI Centre – Balance and Glorious Health

BAGUA AREA 5

The magic square area 5 is the Taiji centre. Its element is earth and is associated with the youngest daughter, a carefree and playful energy. It is connected with, and influenced by, the eight areas surrounding it. The Taiji centre represents the core of your home, your essence, and your life force, or kundalini, which lies in your Earth Star chakra, from whence it rises along your spine as you elevate your own frequencies.

The Taiji centre is about your health and harmony. It symbolizes balance within you and your life. It is your centre. Traditionally, this area represents yourself, and on my 5D Bagua of Higher Aspirations, I have called it Balance and Glorious Health.

I have given this bagua area the colour platinum, like the fifth-dimensional base chakra, because the two chambers of this centre have the task of bringing your masculine and feminine energy into balance. It also has a yin and yang symbol.

The traditional bagua is represented as an octagon with eight sections (trigrams) surrounding the yin and yang symbol in the Taiji centre. Each of the other eight areas directly affects the centre. Each aspect of your life affects you and the frequency of your vibration. When all eight areas are in harmony, the centre will also have the perfect balance of yin and yang energies. In your life, this will translate as good fortune. All that exists in the universe is governed by the yin and yang principles, the divine feminine and masculine energies, and when they are balanced, they bring harmony and good health and activate your potential.

The centre of your home should be clear of furniture so the energy can flow freely, just as it should in your physical body. In my home, it falls into the corridor. There is no furniture, but the wall has a little protrusion. I placed a beautiful bronze candle holder exactly in the centre of the Taiji area without knowing that it was the centre. Again, this is perfect, and nothing needs to be done.

In the living room, where I have decided to activate all bagua areas, I had previously anchored an ascension column into the middle of the room. That means there is a constant flow of high-frequency ascension energies and flames. I would definitely recommend doing this in one of your rooms as well. Because the centre is so important, I felt activating it in more than one room is beneficial. The bedroom is my next choice. So please have a look at where your centre area is and let's clear and activate it.

Next, I will give you three different options on what you can do to activate your Taiji area. Decide which option you want to go for in the various points where you want to activate the Taiji centre. The options came to me as I sat down in each area.

First Option: Call in an etheric, faceted, clear quartz crystal cluster to float in the area and keep the frequencies high. You can, of course, also place real crystals and ask them to keep the energies high.

Second Option: Anchor an ascension column with the help of Ascended Master Serapis Bey, Keeper of the Ascension Flame in the Temple of Luxor. The Ascension Flame will keep the space and your energy field clear and accelerate your ascension journey.

These two options are in the visualization below, but first, let me introduce you to Ascended Master Serapis Bey and explain what an ascension column is.

Meet Ascended Master Serapis Bey

Ascended Master Serapis Bey holds an important role in the ascension process of Earth. He is the Keeper of the Pure White Flame of Ascension. He was a great priest avatar in Atlantis, and his spiritual retreat is the Ascension Temple of Luxor, which is an etheric structure superimposed over the physical remains in Egypt. He is often referred to as

"The Egyptian" because of his involvement with building the pyramids and his strongly felt presence in Egypt.

What Is an Ascension Column?

An ascension column is a column of light in which the ascension flame is anchored and burns permanently. You can ask for your ascension column to be connected to the Ascension Temple in Luxor. Anchoring an ascension column renders a space sacred, and sitting in it will purify your energy fields and accelerate your personal ascension.

Tips on How to Interact with Ascended Master Serapis Bey

- When I tuned in to Ascended Master Serapis Bey to get some inspiration on what tips to give, the first thing he shared with me is that he likes to laugh. He has a great sense of humour, so when connecting with Serapis Bey, smile, and he will be very pleased. I will always remember when he asked me to draw him. I couldn't believe that he made such a request, but I started sketching quickly without much thought, and I was quite surprised by the result. When I tried again later to do it for "real," I wasn't succeeding. That first attempt was special, and I still have the drawing.
- You can ask Serapis Bey to send the Pure White Flame of Ascension to a place in the world where purification and higher consciousness are required, and visualize this happening.
- You can ask Serapis Bey to place the Pure White Flame of Ascension around you and clear you at a deep cellular level.

VISUALIZATION to Clear the Taiji Centre and Activate It with a Crystal or an Ascension Column

1. Sit in the space representing the Taiji area in your home, or wherever you want to activate it.
2. You may wish to light a candle and burn some incense.
3. Close your eyes and relax. Take a few deep breaths into your heart.

4. Set the intention to clear this area, raise the energy, and increase the frequency of vibration.
5. Call the angel of your home to supervise and hold the light. Call your guardian angel and your personal unicorn and dragon to come close.
6. Ask your dragon to blaze flames to clear the area. See this happening.
7. Ask your unicorn to fill the area with pure unicorn light and see the unicorn wafting its horn to spread pure high-frequency light.
8. Ask the angel of your home to fill the area with light, and add love from your heart.
   Become aware of the free-flowing energies where you are sitting, and choose one of the following options:

   • **Option 1:** Call in an etheric crystal to come into this space. See the crystal appear, and ask it whether it would be willing to stay here and take on the task of keeping the frequency high in this spot. Listen to the crystal's answer, and thank it for the service work.

   • **Option 2:** Call in Ascended Master Serapis Bey, and ask him to anchor an ascension column in this space and connect it with the Ascension Flame that burns in his Ascension Temple in Luxor. See a large column of light appearing in your space and see pure white Ascension Flames burn within it.

9. Send gratitude to your angels, unicorn, dragon, and the higher beings that have assisted.
10. Come back with your consciousness into your physical body, and open your eyes.

Third Option – Create a Portal of Light

The third option is an interesting intuition that came to me, and I am about to do it to activate the Taiji centre in my bedroom. I feel guided to open an angel portal here, where high-frequency beings can visit and share their wisdom and inspiration at night when I sleep. I envisage the column to contain energies that help me get refreshing sleep and healing, allowing me to travel in my spirit body into the higher dimension.

I also intend for the portal to link me with high-frequency energies and certain stars and planets holding amazing light, wisdom, and cosmic qualities. Having such a portal in your space will add light to your energy fields and accelerate your ascension path. Many archangels will assist in creating this portal, so let me introduce the ones you haven't met yet.

Meet Archangel Jophiel

Archangel Jophiel is the angel of wisdom and illumination and presents himself with a gentle, pale-golden light. He can direct flashes of inspiration and higher consciousness into your mind. When you connect with his energy, you can access cosmic wisdom and have wonderful ideas. He is also known as the angel of education. Archangel Jophiel is in charge of developing humanity's crown chakras at a fifth-dimensional level. He encourages people to connect with the stars. Archangel Jophiel's spiritual retreat is in the mountains near the Great Wall in northern China. His twin flame is Archangel Christine.

Tips on How to Interact with Archangels Jophiel and Christine

- Connect with Archangel Jophiel by thinking or saying his name and visualizing his gentle, pale-golden light.
- You can ask Archangel Jophiel and his angels to fly over the world and bring inspiration to all schoolchildren.
- Ask Archangel Jophiel for a download of the keys and codes of wisdom.

- Say the affirmation "I AM Archangel Jophiel" to draw his beautiful qualities to you.
- You can ask your spirit to visit Archangel Jophiel's spiritual retreat when you sleep in order to help you learn and acquire wisdom.
- Call upon Archangel Jophiel to clear your crown chakra so that its thousand petals can open, allowing you to connect with the wisdom of the stars.
- If you have citrine, you can use it to connect with Archangel Jophiel. Citrine is Archangel Jophiel's energy solidified.
- You can ask Archangel Jophiel to connect your mind with the mind of Source and beautify your thoughts.
- I often send Archangel Jophiel to school with my daughter to help her with tests.
- Invoke Archangel Christine and ask her to bless you with divine feminine wisdom (this is also very beneficial for men).

Meet Archangel Mary

Archangel Mary is a vast universal angel, meaning that she works not only in our universe but also in others. Her highest-frequency colour is aquamarine, and her light has a wavelike quality. Her Earth mission is to radiate unconditional love and compassion to open and heal the hearts of all people. You feel loved and nurtured when she enfolds you with divine feminine energy. Archangel Mary usually travels with unicorns, and her healing work is very important right now. Archangel Mary's twin flame is Archangel Raphael. Her spiritual retreat is in Lourdes, France.

Tips on How to Interact with Archangel Mary

- Connect with Archangel Mary by thinking or saying her name and visualizing her beautiful, healing aquamarine light.
- You can ask Archangel Mary and her unicorns to fly over the world and bring healing and nurturing to those in need.

- You can say a prayer for someone who is ill: "Beloved Archangel Mary, under grace, I pray for the healing and highest good of (add name). So be it." Visualize Archangel Mary enfolding that person with her aquamarine cloak.
- Ask Archangel Mary to help you open your heart and connect to the love in the cosmos.
- Say the affirmation "I AM Archangel Mary" to draw her beautiful qualities of love and compassion to you.
- You can ask your spirit to visit Archangel Mary's spiritual retreat in Lourdes at night when you sleep to receive healing.

Meet Archangel Sandalphon

Archangel Sandalphon comes with a silvery light. He is a tall angel because his energy reaches from Earth right up to Source. He is also the angel of music and oversees the power of sound in the universe. Archangel Sandalphon is in charge of the Earth Star chakra and can help you ground deeply into the earth and unfold your spiritual potential for this lifetime. His spiritual retreat is in a magical crystal cave at Lake Atitlan, Guatemala. Archangel Sandalphon is referred to as "he" even though he carries divine feminine energy. His divine masculine counterpart is Archangel Metatron.

Tips on How to Interact with Archangel Sandalphon

- Connect with Archangel Sandalphon by thinking or saying his name and visualizing his beautiful silver light.
- You can ask Archangel Sandalphon to help you ground deeply into the earth.
- Ask Archangel Sandalphon to help you unleash your potential.
- Say the affirmation "I AM Archangel Sandalphon" to draw his beautiful qualities to you.
- You can ask your spirit to visit Archangel Sandalphon's crystal cave at night when you sleep to receive his teachings.

- Call upon Archangel Sandalphon to clear your Earth Star chakra and help you create a solid foundation for your lifetime.

Meet Archangel Zadkiel

Archangel Zadkiel appears in a strong violet light. He is the archangel that oversees the Violet Flame together with St. Germain. When you connect with his energy, you can release the past and help the planet to do the same. He brings transformation and karmic release. He is in charge of developing the Soul Star chakra for humanity. His spiritual retreat is above Cuba. His twin flame is Archangel Amethyst.

Tips on How to Interact with Archangels Zadkiel and Amethyst

Connect with Archangel Zadkiel by thinking or saying his name and visualizing his beautiful, violet light, which has the power of transmutation.

- You can ask Archangel Zadkiel to send the gold and silver violet flame dragons to fly over the world and transmute any dense energies into a higher loving vibration.
- Ask Archangel Zadkiel for a download of the keys and codes of freedom.
- Say the affirmation "I AM Archangel Zadkiel" to draw his beautiful qualities to you.
- You can ask your spirit to visit Archangel Zadkiel's spiritual retreat at night when you sleep to receive healing.
- Call upon Archangels Zadkiel and Amethyst to clear your energy fields and bring you healing.
- If you have an amethyst crystal, you can use it to connect with Archangel Amethyst. The amethyst is her energy solidified, and it can help you release the old that no longer serves you in a gentle way.

Cosmic Diamond Violet Flame Note

The Cosmic Diamond Violet Flame is an upgrade of the Gold and Silver Violet Flame. It contains Archangel Gabriel's diamond light, with its power to cut away old and unwanted energies, while bringing clarity and illumination and raising any situation to the fifth dimension or higher.

VISUALIZATION to Activate Your Taiji Centre with a Portal of Light

1. Sit in the space where you want to activate the Taiji centre.
2. You may wish to light a candle and burn some incense.
3. Close your eyes and relax. Take a few deep breaths into your heart.
4. Set the intention to clear this area and anchor a column of light to connect you with cosmic energies, certain stars or planets, and higher beings like ascended masters, angels, unicorns, and galactic dragons and allow you to travel in your spirit body.
5. Call your angel of the home, guardian angel, and personal unicorn and dragon to come close.
6. Ask your dragon to clear the area with its blazing flames, and observe as it carries out its work.
7. Ask your unicorn to pour light into your crown chakra to open its petals. This will help you establish cosmic links.
8. Focus on the spot where you want to create the portal, and visualize a column of light descending from the heavens and anchoring deep into the planet below your home.
9. Invoke Archangel Michael to add his blue energy to the column, and see him fill it with protection, power, strength, determination, and courage.
10. Invoke Archangel Chamuel to add his pink light to the column, and see him filling it with love and compassion. This light will help you keep your heart open and aligned with the frequency of love.

11. Invoke Archangel Jophiel to add his golden light and the divine quality of wisdom to the column. His energy will inspire you.

12. Invoke Archangel Gabriel and Zadkiel to add their light and the Cosmic Diamond Violet Flame. This will ensure the energies stay clear and pure and bring you transformation.

13. Invoke Archangel Raphael to add his emerald-green light. It will ensure a constant flow of abundance and healing energy coming your way and support your health.

14. Invoke Archangel Mary to add her aquamarine light, which contains love, healing, compassion, and nurturing.

15. Ask your unicorn to add its light.

16. Ask your dragon to add its energy and flames to protect the portal.

17. Invoke any other energies or higher beings you would like to add light, and see that happen.

18. Invoke Archangel Sandalphon, and ask him to ground the portal into the earth. Ask for the portal to remain as long as it is useful to you.

19. Ask Archangel Michael to place one of his angels by the portal to protect it.

20. Send gratitude to the angels, unicorn, dragon, and higher beings that have assisted.

21. Come back with your consciousness into your physical body, and open your eyes.

Your Health

You have seen that the Taiji Centre is connected with your health on all levels: physical, emotional, mental, and spiritual. So the last part of this chapter is a visualization to restore your health to its divine glory and balance your masculine and feminine energies. Even if you have ailments, always think and affirm that you radiate perfect health on all levels. We will work with Diana Cooper's 12 chakra system, introduced to you in week 4, the 11D Energy of Regeneration from Helios, and the yin and yang dragons, which have the power to balance you and the world.

11D Energy of Regeneration from Helios Note

The golden-orange 11D Energy of Regeneration from Helios is a new high-frequency cosmic energy available to us. Helios is the Great Central Sun, the sun beyond our sun, and this awesome energy holds your highest potential, codes of regeneration, and happiness. It can heal and energize your chakras and glands, boost your immune system, increase the light you carry, and break up mental and emotional patterns that no longer serve you. It can also help your pituitary gland to produce rejuvenating hormones and promote eternal youth. As you absorb the energy into every cell of your body, it helps you build your crystalline lightbody for the new Golden Age, and it encourages you to feel at one with Earth and Source and to be a bridge for a new way of being, where you are anchored deep into the planet and residing with your consciousness in the 7th dimension.

Tips on How to Use the 11D Energy of Regeneration from Helios

I am sharing some example invocations:

- "I now invoke with love the 11D Energy of Regeneration from Helios to flow through me to activate my highest potential."
- "I now invoke with love the 11D Energy of Regeneration from Helios into my third eye and pituitary gland and ask it to produce only rejuvenating hormones." This helps you to hold a vision of eternal life and immortality.
- "I now invoke with love the 11D Energy of Regeneration from Helios to break up any mental and emotional patterns that no longer serve me." If you know what they are, you can name them.

- "I now invoke with love the 11D Energy of Regeneration from Helios to flow through my chakra column and anchor into our planet." To be a channel for the 11D Energy of Regeneration from Helios is important service work and accelerates Earth's ascension process.
- "I now invoke with love the 11D Energy of Regeneration to flow through all my cells and activate happiness."

Yin and Yang Dragons Note

The yin dragon carries the divine feminine vibration of the universe, and the yang dragon carries the divine masculine vibration of the universe, and they are mighty ninth-dimensional beings. Regardless of gender, you have divine feminine and masculine energies within you. The yin and yang dragons can help you balance them.

When the feminine and masculine energies come into equilibrium in your base chakra, your potential and power increase, allowing you to live in a grounded and balanced way on the planet. The yin dragon appears in a soft, loving, and nurturing silvery-white light. The yang dragon has a dark but beautifully shimmering aura exuding power and strength.

Tips on How to Interact with the Yin and Yang Dragons

- Simply ask the yin and yang dragons to bless you.
- Invoke the yin and yang dragons, and ask them to balance your energies. See the two dragons streaming their light into you. As the white and dark mingle, it becomes beautiful shimmering silver. See it flowing down your chakra column until it reaches the base.
- Ask the yin and yang dragons to radiate their light onto the world to create divine balance, and visualize that happening.
- Express your gratitude to these mighty beings.

VISUALIZATION to Restore Balance and Glorious Health

1. Sit in your Taiji centre. Close your eyes and relax.

2. Imagine that your Taiji centre is a beautiful garden with plants, trees, flowers, bodies of water, crystals, colourful birds, butterflies, and whatever comes to your mind. Let your inspiration flow, and create your own personal paradise with your imagination. As you look up into the sky, you can see both the sun and the moon bathing you with their light.

3. Take some time to explore your garden with your guardian angel, unicorn, and dragon and then choose a comfortable place to rest.

4. Invoke the golden-orange 11D Energy of Regeneration from Helios to descend, and see it flowing into your golden Stellar Gateway chakra about one meter above your head. The Stellar Gateway is your portal into the sixth dimension and above. It connects you with your highest dimensional aspect, the Monad, also known as your I AM Presence.

5. See the golden-orange energy flowing into your Soul Star chakra about 50 centimetres above your head and merging with its magenta energy. This chakra helps you embody your soul and activate your unique gifts.

6. See the 11D Energy of Regeneration from Helios flowing into your moon-white causal chakra above your head, ensuring a clear connection with the higher realms and the angels, dragons, and unicorns.

7. The 11D Energy of Regeneration from Helios flows into your crystal-clear crown chakra, allowing you to receive cosmic downloads and nourishing your wisdom. Next, the 11D Energy of Regeneration from Helios flows into the little pinecone-shaped pineal gland below the crown chakra to expand your consciousness.

8. See the golden-orange energy flow into your crystal-clear third eye, helping you see from a higher and divine perspective. Next, it flows into the pea-sized pituitary gland behind the third eye. Ask this gland now to produce rejuvenating hormones for you.

9. The 11D Energy of Regeneration from Helios flows into your throat chakra. See the golden-orange light merge with the electric blue of your throat chakra, allowing you to speak your truth with love. Next, the golden-orange energy flows into the butterfly-shaped thyroid gland.

10. The golden-orange 11D Energy of Regeneration from Helios flows into your pure white heart chakra, opening you up to higher love. Next, it flows into the thymus gland, shaped like a thyme leaf above your heart, to boost your immune system.

11. The 11D Energy of Regeneration from Helios flows into your golden solar plexus, allowing only fifth-dimensional loving energies to enter. Next, it flows into the pear-shaped pancreas.

12. The 11D Energy of Regeneration from Helios flows into the orange navel chakra. When this is activated in the fifth dimension, you connect lovingly and joyfully with all your fellow brothers and sisters. You understand oneness.

13. The golden-orange light floods your pink sacral chakra, opening you up to transcendent love and caring for people. Next, it bathes your reproductive organs.

14. The 11D Energy of Regeneration from Helios flows into the base chakra. See how the golden-orange energy merges with the platinum of the base chakra. **In this centre, the masculine and feminine energies come into equilibrium, allowing you to live in a grounded and balanced way on the planet.** Next, the 11D Energy of Regeneration from Helios bathes the adrenal glands.

15. The 11D Energy of Regeneration from Helios flows into the Earth Star chakra below your feet. Visualize the golden-orange light merging with the silvery light of the Earth Star. See silvery roots growing from the bottom of your feet all the way down into the centre of Mother Earth. The deeper the roots, the higher the tree can reach.

16. Visualize the golden-orange 11D Energy of Regeneration from Helios, together with the powerful fifth-dimensional light from your chakras, flooding your physical body, illuminating your cells, the 12 strands of DNA within them, and your organs and bones. Focus this incredible healing force on any part of your body that needs it right now, and hear your cells communicate the message of perfect health to each other.

17. Ask the energy to flood your emotional and mental bodies, aligning your feelings and thoughts with the Divine. Your feelings are high-frequency, and your thoughts are positive and noble. They are thoughts that move you forward on your path.

18. Ask the 11D Energy of Regeneration from Helios to flood your spiritual bodies all the way up through the dimensions, and see your aura lighting up with high-frequency light and colours.

19. Once more, look up into the sky at the sun and the moon. Feel how the golden-orange sunlight and silvery moonlight balance the divine masculine and feminine energies in your fields. With your mind's eye, see the sun and the moon merge and transform into a yin and yang symbol in the sky. It is the most beautiful yin and yang symbol you have ever seen, sparkling and shimmering with vibrant light.

20. Become aware of two dragons flying in the sky in front of the symbol. They are the yin and yang dragons. The yin dragon radiates a loving silvery-white light, and she flies in front of

the dark yang area of the symbol. The yang dragon has a dark but beautifully shimmering aura and flies in front of the white yin area of the heavenly sign. He exudes masculine power and strength. See the two dragons embracing each other. The white energy enfolds the dark dragon, and the dark shimmering energy enfolds the white dragon while they flap their wings. The dragons radiate beautiful shimmering silvery light, which pours powerfully into your aura and chakra column, establishing perfect harmony and balance within you.

21. Take a deep breath and then exhale towards the sky. A rainbow appears, showing you how blessed you are. Send gratitude to Source for your glorious divine health, and be open to amazing things happening in your life.

22. Thank the yin and yang dragons, and see them fly away.

23. Bring your consciousness fully back into your physical body. Feel the ground firmly below your feet. Open your eyes, and expect miracles.

CONNECT with the Number Five

The number five is about change and transformation. Its influence helps you expand and move onto a higher path. It is dynamic and brings the qualities of freedom, adventure, and wisdom.

1. Close your eyes, and take a deep breath.

2. Once more, you connect with the cosmic turtle rising from the Luo River. Five dots are mysteriously glowing on its back.

3. Allow the turtle to transport you to the ninth-dimensional cosmic pool of the number five. Together with the turtle, immerse yourself in the energies.

4. Let them stream into you and help you transform into a glorious being with perfect divine health. Feel the freedom this brings you.

5. You are feeling courageous, excited, adventurous, and dynamic.

6. The energy is bathing you with the wisdom to use these qualities for your highest path.

7. Send your gratitude to the turtle for the expansion it brought you and return safely to your space.

Intention for the Taiji Area of Your Life

"My divine masculine and feminine energies are balanced, and I radiate perfect divine health."

Please repeat this affirmation for the coming week, or write your own for the Taiji area.

QIAN – Incredible Higher Support

BAGUA AREA 6

This area of your bagua is called Qian. The energy of the Qian area is yang/yang/yang, and it is associated with the energy of the father, being powerful and in charge, acting with integrity, and having great wisdom. Qian symbolizes heaven, and its element is metal. Qian traditionally represents helpful people. On my 5D Bagua of Higher Aspirations, I have called it Incredible Higher Support.

I have given this bagua area the colour blue, like the sky and the heavens. I felt that blue is perfect, because it is also associated with the Archangel Michael and the protective divine masculine power this warrior angel represents.

In fact, Qian is a strongly yang energy, the divine masculine, the heavenly father, and an expansive and creative celestial force. On an earthly level, this area is about friends and supportive people in your life. It is family and community-orientated and connected with good karma. If you do good and care, then you will experience people being helpful and generous towards you. It is also about the synchronicities in life, when you know things were just meant to happen. The area is also connected with travel—physical travel and travel in your spirit body to other dimensions.

You also have a support team available on a heavenly level. Like everyone on Earth, you are on the ascension path, whether you consciously know it or not. To move forward on this path, you have an amazing team of helpers supporting you each step of the way. Your ascension team comprises your guardian angel, unicorn, dragon, goddesses, and ascended masters. You have already received the names of your unicorn and dragons, and in this chapter, you will engage more closely with your guardian angel and your overlighting archangel.

First, let's have a look at the Qian area. In my home, it falls onto the kitchen, literally where we cook. It feels like the symbolism is good. Cooking is about nurturing and nourishing. When we care for and nurture people and higher beings, the law of karma will ensure that we receive the same in turn. Believe it or not, there are "cooking angels." You can call on them to inspire you with creative cooking. I also have a routine of sending healing love and light to people who need it every morning. I send love and light to all the kingdoms of Earth, minerals, nature, elemental beings, animals, and all of humanity. I send gratitude and blessings to Source, the ascended masters, angels, unicorns, and dragons.

I will also activate this area in my living room. It falls onto the corner that leads into the corridor (without a door). I feel I need to add something here. Wind chimes are the answer. I wonder whether I can get the same ones I already have by the entrance; they would be hanging opposite each other, and the flow of *qi* (chi) would go from one to the other. The bookshelves here mostly contain my children's books, belongings, and photos. Still, part of one of my bookshelves is also in this area, containing my spiritual books and crystals, and I have just added an image representing my guardian angel here.

Interestingly, it is also the area where I always burn incense, so it is constantly being purified. I have also told my daughter to give the bookshelf a good clearing. Now, go and look at where your Qian area falls and let's clear it.

VISUALIZATION to Clear the Qian Area

1. Sit in the space that represents the Qian area in your home.
2. You may wish to light a candle and burn some incense.
3. Close your eyes and relax. Take a few deep breaths into your heart, and feel it expand.

4. Set the intention to clear this area, raise the energy to the seventh dimension, and beautify and strengthen your connection with people and higher beings.

5. Call your angel of the home to supervise and hold the light. Call your guardian angel and your personal unicorn and dragon to come close.

6. Ask your personal dragon to clear this space with its flames.

7. Ask your unicorn to add beautiful pearlescent-white light.

8. Ask your guardian angel to fill the area with their light and bless it with their qualities and energy.

9. Reflect on whether there is anything else to be done in this area. Should you remove or add things? You can ask the angel of your home and your guardian angel for advice.

10. Thank the angels, dragon, and unicorn for the work carried out.

11. Come back with your consciousness into your physical body and open your eyes.

I trust you have made the necessary changes. I have bought another set of golden bell wind chimes, and I feel that they brought balance to the space and ensured a good flow of energy. Now, let's focus on your guardian angel and find out their name, but first read the guardian angel note.

Guardian Angel Note

Your guardian angel is your most loyal companion, because they have been with you throughout all your incarnations from aeons ago; they profoundly enhance your life. You already know that angels are androgynous, but your guardian angel will present themselves as more feminine or masculine, depending on what supports you best and connects with you through your open heart.

Your guardian angel holds your divine blueprint and guides you towards your soul purpose. They know who you truly are, your gifts, talents, and full potential. You and your guardian angel evolve together, and they celebrate all your achievements with you. When you raise your frequency, your guardian angel can also raise their own. One of my angel students, Nicolò, pointed out that when we work on ourselves and do visualizations to raise our consciousness, we give our guardian angel the opportunity to visit the higher dimension. So if, during a visualization, we only access the 12th dimension for a moment, your guardian angel will be with you.

Your guardian angel will be happiest when you talk to them daily and give them jobs. They can help you with anything. All you must do is ask clearly. You accelerate the process by consciously collaborating with your guardian angel to bring forth your divine blueprint. They will whisper the highest choices to you, and it is then up to you to follow or take some more time. I feel immense gratitude when thinking about my guardian angel Wuji. When I say his name, I get a sense of birds singing, the sky clearing, and the sun breaking through. Knowing that he is always with me for eternity is such a blessing directly from the heart of Source. Knowing he will step close by when I need him makes me feel empowered, loved, and safe.

Tips on How to Interact with Your Guardian Angel

- Make it a habit to invoke your guardian angel every day. Greet them, and ask them to support you throughout the day.
- Tell your guardian angel that you love them, and feel their love flowing into your heart.
- Ask your guardian angel to help you rise above any problems. When you do that, the answers will present themselves and the challenge will dissolve.
- Talk to your guardian angel and all higher beings using only positive high-frequency words. All your communications are like prayers, and your guardian angel can then work for your highest good. Expect miracles.
- Express gratitude: "Beloved Guardian Angel, thank you for being my guardian angel."

- Your guardian angel evolves with you, so you can enthusiastically say: "Guardian Angel (use their name), let's raise our frequencies today!"
- Breathe in love and joy, and ask your guardian angel to touch your aura and make it golden.
- Once you know your guardian angel's name, sing it. It will greatly enhance your connection.
- If a challenging person is in your life, you can ask your guardian angel to deliver a loving message. They will talk to the other person's guardian angel and send blessings to resolve the issue. To help this process, imagine the other person receiving your loving message for the highest good.

VISUALIZATION to Receive Your Guardian Angel's Name

It is time to find out your guardian angel's name. When you ask, accept whatever name you are given, trusting that its vibration is perfect. I have already explained that angels are androgynous, and you may perceive them as a more male or female presence. For ease, I will refer to the guardian angel as "they" throughout the visualization.

1. Sit in the Qian area of your home.
2. Close your eyes, and breathe gently. Get really comfortable in your seat, and allow yourself to relax deeper and deeper with each breath you take.
3. Visualize yourself standing on a beach of soft white sand in a magnificent bay. In front of you, the blue sea shimmers and glints in the golden sunshine, with the waves gently lapping on the shore. The bay is composed of rocks and cliffs on each side.
4. As you walk along the beach, you notice footprints in the sand. You follow them. They are leading towards some rocks at the end of the bay. The footprints continue along a sandy pathway lined with wild seaside flowers and other fragrant plants.

5. You now find yourself at the entrance to a large cave. You enter the cave. It is a womb-like space, and you feel safe and secure as you move forward towards a beautiful golden light. You sense that there is a radiant being of light in front of you.

6. Notice how much lighter you begin to feel. Feel your heart opening like a flower in the sun, accepting the love emanating from this wonderful being. You just know that this is your guardian angel.

7. Your guardian angel welcomes you warmly, and you sense their familiar, loving energy around you. Take a moment to observe this wondrous being, and smile.

8. Your guardian angel steps close and invites you to move into their arms, enfolding you with their immense wings, and embracing you with love, light, and joy. You feel moved, and your heart is opening wider.

9. Your angel wants you to know that they love you unconditionally, every moment, forever and eternally, no matter what you do. They are always here to love and support you, helping you find loving and wise solutions for every situation. Take a moment to express your gratitude for their being with you always.

10. You now have the opportunity to ask your guardian angel's name. Ask them to drop it into your mind now.

11. Accept whatever name you are given. Trust that this is the name your angel would like you to use when communicating with them. It has the perfect vibration. If you didn't get a name, trust it will come to you later. You may read or hear a name and intuitively know that this is it.

12. Thank your guardian angel for this wonderful opportunity. Bring your awareness back to your physical body, and when you feel ready, open your eyes.

Archangels

Now that you have deepened your connection with your guardian angel, we will focus on archangels. They are mighty beings that oversee big projects of light, such as developing the fifth-dimensional chakras for humanity. Archangels are in charge of angels and guardian angels and allocate specific tasks to them. They can transmit divine blessings and qualities to you, and you can connect with all of them.

Intuitively, you will connect with the archangel whose energy can help you at any given moment, but you will have one archangel to whom you feel very connected. This is your overlighting archangel. Your energy vibration is attuned to theirs. By radiating their qualities, you work for this archangel and they work through you to have an impact on others. However, it is still beneficial to integrate the qualities of all archangels. Each archangel has a twin flame with divine feminine energies. In the past, humanity has tended to give importance to the masculine aspect, but right now, to bring divine balance to Earth, the divine feminine is returning, and therefore, honouring the divine feminine is essential. You already have met several archangels in this book, but before we do the next visualization, let me introduce you to one more.

Meet Archangel Uriel

Archangel Uriel presents himself with a magnificent, deep-golden light. He radiates peace and wisdom. When you connect with him, you can release any lower energies and transmute them into love. You feel confident and stand in your power. Archangel Uriel is in charge of the development of the fifth-dimensional solar plexus of humanity, and his spiritual retreat is above the Tatra mountains in Poland. His twin flame is Archangel Aurora.

Tips on How to Interact with Archangels Uriel and Aurora

- Thinking of Archangel Uriel or calling his name will draw his light to you, and you can attune to his energy.

- Ask Archangel Uriel to fill you with peace and wisdom.
- Ask Archangel Uriel to enfold you in his immense wings, and see your solar plexus radiate a magnificent golden light, filling you with power and confidence.
- You can pray: "Beloved Archangel Uriel, please help me feel more confident."
- Say the affirmation "I AM Archangel Uriel." I AM affirmations are powerful because they draw to you what you are affirming. If you say "I AM Archangel Uriel," your highest-dimensional aspect merges with Archangel Uriel, and you draw his amazing qualities to you.
- Ask Archangels Uriel and Aurora to help you move forward on your ascension path with confidence.
- Ask Archangel Aurora to help you with new beginnings and bless your projects.

VISUALIZATION to Visit Your Overlighting Archangel

1. Sit in the space that represents the Qian area in your home. Close your eyes, and breathe deeply.
2. Call your guardian angel by their name, and smile. Ask them to come close. They will take you on a journey to meet your overlighting archangel. Set this intention. Your guardian angel moves behind you and places the palm of their hand on the upper part of your back. Feel their energy flowing into your back and spine. Then they come back in front of you and embrace you. Feel their energy merging with yours. Become aware of them unfolding their beautiful wings and starting to flap them. As you observe this in wonder, you feel your own wings growing on your back. Unfurl them, and start moving them. Become acquainted with how they feel.
3. Your guardian angel takes you up into the sky and encourages you to use your own wings to fly. As you become more confident, they release their embrace, and you fly freely.

4. You are journeying through the fifth dimension, and now you are soaring up into the sixth and the seventh dimensions.

5. As you align your vibration to this dimension, you marvel at the beautiful light and colours around you. Your guardian angel takes you to solid-looking ground where you can see various temples built in harmonious shapes and colours. The site is covered in blooming trees and beautiful, vibrant flowers. They look well tended and loved, and their fragrant scents reach you as you breathe in.

6. Your guardian angel explains that this is a training establishment for guardian angels. Each of the major archangels has a temple here. Your guardian angel mentions some of their names: Gabriel, Uriel, Chamuel, Michael, Raphael, Metatron, Mary, and maybe others. Which one attracts you? The one that resonates will likely be the same archangel your guardian angel trained with.

7. Your guardian angel is leading you along a sand-coloured path to the temple where they trained. You are standing in front of the doors. What colour is the temple? What does the sign above the door say? (Training School of Archangel . . . ?) Let the name drop into your mind.

8. Your guardian angel knocks, and an angel opens the door. Follow your guardian angel into the temple. They know their way around and take you to the archangel's teaching hall. They quietly open the door and gesture for you to follow them in.

9. You see angels seated, listening to the teaching of the archangel in front of them. In this teaching hall, the guardian angels learn how to be companions to humans and guide them through their lives with love. Here, they learn how to hold the vision of their human's divine blueprint, remain by their side at all times, and hold them in unconditional love. Here, they learn to radiate the same qualities as their archangel and pass them on to their human ward.

10. Take a moment to observe the archangel. What colour light do they emanate? What divine qualities do they radiate?

What are they saying? You may not hear the words but can tune in to the energy.

11. The archangel finishes their talk, and the guardian angel trainees start to leave the teaching hall. The archangel approaches you and your guardian angel and greets them like an old friend. Then the archangel raises their gaze to look at you. They smile warmly, and their eyes lock with yours.

12. The archangel shows you the palm of their hand, and you see a blazing flame. It looks spectacular. Take note of the colour. This is your archangel's essence flame. With your permission, the archangel places the palm of their hand on your chest to share their essence with you. Know that by sharing their essence, you will be able to transmit the qualities of your overlighting archangel at a higher level, and you will have a bigger impact on people. You work for this archangel by radiating their qualities, and they work through you.

13. Stay in silence for a few minutes, and let the energy integrate. During this time, you can communicate with the archangel. They may have a message for you. This may be a word, a symbol, or a vision. You can also ask them to bless the heaven area by sending a ray from their hand.

14. It is time to return. Thank the archangel for the gifts and insights you have received, and say goodbye. The archangel thanks you in turn for your service work. Follow your guardian angel out of the temple. As you return, many angels emerge from the other temple doors. Their lessons have finished, and they are returning to their service work.

15. With your guardian angel, walk back along the sand-coloured path, unfold your wings, and come down through the dimensions back into your own space. Bring your awareness fully into your body. Open your eyes with the knowledge that your consciousness has expanded.

Connect with the Number Six

Number six is about sociability and seeking spiritual community. It is family-orientated and brings responsibility, commitment, and self-worth. It carries caring, empathetic, and nurturing energy and helps you see from the heart and with compassion. Number six assists you in being a teacher or healer and helps your creative energies to emerge. It encourages you to have faith and focus on the divine.

1. Close your eyes, and take a deep breath.
2. Visualize the turtle rising from the river water. With wonder, you observe the map on its back. The area with six dots is illuminated.
3. As you see the six glowing dots, the turtle transports you to the ninth-dimensional cosmic origin of this number.
4. As you bathe in the pool of number six, you see yourself living in a community with your soul family. Everyone, including yourself, is supportive and caring, seeing and acting from the heart.
5. The divine qualities of number six are streaming into you, bathing you with the energy of responsibility, commitment, empathy, and compassion.
6. Allow the turtle to return you safely to Earth, and express your gratitude for the support it brought you.

Intention for the Qian Area of Your Life

You have now met more components of your ascension team and will know just how powerfully supported you are. This week's intention is:

"I call upon my amazing ascension team to support me on my path, and I integrate the qualities of all archangels."

Or you can write a different one that resonates with you.

DUI – Never-Ending Creativity

BAGUA AREA 7

This area of your bagua is called Dui. The energy of the Dui area is yin/yang/yang, and it is associated with the energy of the youngest daughter: playful, romantic, new relationships, and harvest time. Dui is symbolized by a lake, and its element is metal. Dui traditionally represents children. On my 5D Bagua of Higher Aspirations, I have called it Never-Ending Creativity.

I have given this bagua area a warm, bright-orange colour like the fifth-dimensional navel chakra. The navel and sacral chakra are associated with expressing your creativity for the highest good.

The Dui area is about children and creativity. Children are creative, playful, spontaneous, and lively, bringing action and vitality to a family, as well as happiness, joy, and satisfaction. The Dui area is also associated with having an idea, making it into a project, and completing it. Ideas are the "children" of your mind. The Dui area concerns your creative projects, inspirations, or even business products. You bring inspiration down into the depths of the lake, where it is nurtured like a seed. The lake symbolizes your inner realm. Creativity emerges from deep within you. From the bottom of the lake, never-ending creativity comes up. The clear, still lake increases your intuition and offers you ideas and wisdom. It keeps your emotions high. It is a place to be still and allow your creativity to emerge.

I checked out my Dui area, which falls in the kitchen, not where I cook (cooking is associated with creativity) but where the kitchen table stands. The kitchen table is where we prepare food and the children carry out other creative work. There is also a small bookshelf with teaching materials and cooking recipes. So I felt it was good to activate it here, but I will also activate it in my living room.

Interestingly, it falls on the left part of my sofa in the living room, exactly where I meditate and inspiration comes to me. I sit here every morning and channel info for my work and writing. A small, beautiful, decorative glass table with a lamp stands next to the sofa with a bowl containing pebble crystals, keeping the frequency high. There are also journals on the sofa arm and two piles of paper on the floor, not looking very attractive, but each represents a project I am working on (one being this book). I felt that it was okay because it resulted from expressing my creativity. The Ascension column I have anchored in the centre of this room also extends to this area, keeping the energies pure and clear. Now check where your Dui area is, and let's clear and activate it.

VISUALIZATION to Clear the Dui Area

1. Sit in the space that represents the Dui area in your home.
2. You may wish to light a candle and burn some incense.
3. Close your eyes and relax. Take a few deep breaths into your heart, and feel it expand.
4. Set the intention to clear this area, raise the energy, and increase the flow of inspiration and creativity in your life.
5. Call your angel of the home to supervise and hold the light. Call your guardian angel and your personal unicorn and dragon to come close.
6. Ask your personal dragon to clear this space with its flames.
7. Ask your unicorn to add beautiful pearlescent-white light to this area.
8. Below the space you are sitting, imagine an underground lake with the clearest water you have ever seen. Like all water, it carries love, and a water dragon keeps it clear and pure. But this water has a special property: It nurtures the seeds of your ideas and makes them grow.

9. Reflect on whether there is anything else to be done in this area. Should you remove or add things? You can ask your angel of the home and your unicorn and dragon for advice.
10. Thank the angels, dragons, and your unicorn for the work carried out.
11. Come back with your consciousness into your physical body, and open your eyes.

Be Creative

Are you a creative person? Do you have projects that satisfy you? Creativity fills you with motivation and enthusiasm for life. Being always in the flow of inspiration and creativity is a beautiful state. Start a project, complete it, and begin a new one. This is how I live.

Are you working on a project right now? Take a moment and think about how many projects you are working on right now. I am currently doing a business course, creating a teaching module, and working on this book and a novel. Are you a person that starts a project and completes it? Or are you having difficulty doing that? Maybe you start projects and don't finish them? To begin and complete a project is a superpower to be cultivated, because it moves you forward and brings joy to life.

VISUALIZATION to Bring Forth Your Creativity

1. Sit in your Dui area. Close your eyes and relax.
2. Call your angel of the home, your guardian angel, and your personal unicorn and dragon to come close.
3. Take three deep breaths into your heart, and feel the energy expand. Connect with your heart, and think about what kind of project would make your heart sing and your soul rejoice.
4. To help you with that, let's call in Archangel Jophiel. He is the angel of wisdom and inspiration. See Archangel Jophiel arrive in your room. Take time to connect with him and breathe in his wonderful golden energy.

5. Archangel Jophiel now touches your crown chakra with his finger. See your crown chakra opening up like a lotus flower and connecting you with the stars and wisdom of the Universe.

6. Remember also the underground lake of the Dui area, and reach down with your awareness. It increases your intuition and nurtures the seeds of your manifestation. Sit for a few minutes, connected with the heavens above and the earth below, and let inspiration come.

7. The silver-white yin dragon you met in the previous chapter is joining you. She is an amazing sight as she flies into your space and lands beside you. She has come to help you give birth to a project or a new higher path, which might also require a new aspect awakening in you. The silver-white yin dragon breathes into your pink sacral chakra (and womb) to activate it at a higher level and kindle your creativity. Feel this happening.

8. Now, have a chat with the silver-white yin dragon. What does your soul require right now? What kind of project? Speak to the yin dragon about it, and get advice.

9. As your project takes form, the dark, shimmering yang dragon appears. With your permission, he blazes white flames into your orange navel chakra to encourage you to take positive action. Tell the yang dragon what you want to create. See it with your mind's eye, and visualize the dragon breathing into your image so it can come into manifestation.

10. Focus on the underground lake with the clear water below your Dui area. Beautiful shimmering crystals are lining it. See the water dragon that inhabits it moving through the water gracefully, causing a current and flow. The lake water is nurturing the seed you have planted today; see it growing in your mind's eye.

11. Thank Archangel Jophiel for inspiring you and gifting you with beautiful thoughts. Thank the yin and yang dragons for their help, and remember to invoke them daily to assist you with completing your project. They can literally fire you up.

12. Slowly bring back your consciousness into your room and your physical body. Feel the ground firmly below your feet. When you feel ready, open your eyes, feeling enthusiastic and motivated.

CONNECT with the Number Seven

The number seven encourages you to think and become a seeker of knowledge and truth through meditation. It allows you to access higher wisdom and expand your consciousness, moving you forward on your ascension path. It is the number of spirituality.

1. Close your eyes, and take a deep breath.
2. Visualize the turtle rising from the river water. Seven dots are illuminated.
3. On the turtle's back, you are rising to the ninth-dimensional cosmic pool of the number seven out in the universe.
4. As you bathe in this high-frequency energy, you are illuminated and inspired with knowledge and higher spiritual wisdom from the pool and the turtle. Your consciousness expands, and inspiration flows.
5. Allow the energy to stream into you, bathing you with its benefits.
6. Allow the turtle to return you safely to Earth, and express your gratitude for the expansion it brought you.

Intention for the Dui Area of Your Life

"I am full of creativity, and the highest inspiration flows through me. I start and complete projects with enthusiasm, motivation, and great joy."

Please repeat this affirmation for the coming week, or write your own for the Dui area.

GEN – Embodying Your Soul and Accessing Its Wisdom

BAGUA AREA 8

This area of your bagua is called Gen. The energy of the Gen area is yang/yin/yin, and it is associated with the youngest son. It is a motivating and outgoing energy. Gen symbolizes mountain, and its element is earth. Gen traditionally represents knowledge. On my 5D Bagua of Higher Aspirations, I have called it Embodying Your Soul and Accessing Its Wisdom.

I have given this bagua area a vibrant magenta colour like the Soul Star chakra. In this centre, you access your soul wisdom and talents, and it is looked after by Archangel Mariel, who comes with a magenta light.

Gen is associated with learning and knowledge. At a higher level, it is about intuition, awareness of the soul, and accessing its wisdom. The mountain is the perfect place to meditate and cultivate the higher aspects of your being. It is a place of contemplation, tranquillity, and stillness and is perfect for becoming one with your soul. When you activate this area in your home, it will facilitate learning. At a higher level, it will help you embody your soul.

I have discovered that my Gen area is completely missing from my floor plan. The wall behind where it should be has bookshelves all along. This is interesting because books are perfect for the Gen area, but in my case, they are not actually in it but on the border.

I had an idea and called my angel of the home, Dora, to help me sort this out with the following request: "Beloved Dora, please place an etheric mirror along the entire wall to compensate for the missing space. Also, mirror the books of wisdom and learning and the crystals on these bookshelves onto the missing side. Thank you. So be it."

Next, I will activate this area in my living room. The spot where it falls is right next to the entrance. The bookshelf here contains my teaching certificate and books. Interestingly, the books I have written myself are here, along with a diary in which I record only very important spiritual experiences and achievements. The shelf also contains all my bigger crystals, particularly rose quartz, amethyst, apophyllite, morganite, celestite, stilbite, and pink halite. Crystals come to you with a mission and will radiate their qualities for your benefit. They will keep the energy vibration very high and spread their blessings. So please look at your Gen area, and let's clear it.

VISUALIZATION to Clear the Gen Area

1. Sit in the space that represents the Gen area in your home.
2. You may wish to light a candle and burn some incense.
3. Close your eyes and relax. Take a few deep breaths into your heart.
4. Set the intention to clear this area, raise the energy, and increase the flow of learning and acquiring skills that move you forward.
5. Call your angel of the home to supervise and hold the light. You can also call your guardian angel and your personal unicorn and dragon to come close.
6. Imagine that you are sitting in a mountainous area with breathtaking views. You might see majestic birds soaring high.
7. Ask your dragon to clear the area and your unicorn to add its light.
8. Ask your angel of the home to fill this space with light and add your love.
9. Have a chat with your angel, unicorn, and dragon to check whether you need to change anything here.
10. Give thanks for the cleansing and insights.

11. Come back with your consciousness into your physical body, and open your eyes.

Your Evolution and the Soul Merge

Your evolution is like climbing a mountain. As a child, I thought I wouldn't have to learn anymore once school had finished. Later, I found out that's when real learning starts. Now, as a teacher, I know I am constantly learning. My students are also my teachers. Every day is an opportunity to grow and learn, so take a moment to reflect on your present life. Are there any courses you would like to take? Are there any skills you desire to learn?

Every course or skill you learn takes you a step further. It is part of the divine plan for you. Money, children, and time are usually excuses. Nothing is more important than your evolution, because that is why you are here. Earth is a school where you take tests or initiations that expand your consciousness. Have you been putting anything off? Go for it now. Take action.

Schools, universities, and courses are one thing, but you can also learn differently. Believe it or not, you can learn while you meditate or sleep by visiting inner-plane training establishments, spiritual universities, or portals. This morning, I visited the learning temple of Ascended Master Lord Kuthumi in meditation. He is not an ascended master I often consciously connect with, but he happens to be the one who assists people with learning and understanding spiritual truth. He works on the second divine ray that Source beams to Earth, associated with wisdom and education.

In the next visualization, you will journey up a mountain representing your soul's nobility. You will meet Archangel Jophiel again, who is in charge of activating the fifth-dimensional crown chakra for all of humanity, and Archangel Mariel, who is in charge of the Soul Star chakra, which is about 50 centimetres above your head. The activated fifth-dimensional Soul Star chakra connects you with your soul, giving you access to its gifts.

In this visualization, you will hear about the Soul Merge. There are seven major initiations on the ascension path. The third initiation is about developing a level of mastery of your mental body, and when you have completed it, you will experience the Soul Merge. This means that you now embody your soul here on Earth and have access to its gifts and talents. On the inner planes, this is considered the first major initiation. Please read the information about Archangel Mariel and Ascended Master Lord Kuthumi to familiarize yourself with their energy and then do the visualization to accelerate your evolution and embody your soul.

Meet Archangel Mariel

Archangel Mariel radiates divine masculine energies and has a glorious magenta aura. He can help you reconnect with your soul and access the gifts you have acquired on your soul journey. Archangel Mariel and his twin flame, Lavender, are in charge of developing the fifth-dimensional Soul Star chakra (together with Archangels Zadkiel and Amethyst). The spiritual retreat of Archangels Mariel and Zadkiel is above the Himalayas.

Tips on How to Interact with Archangels Mariel and Lavender

- Thinking of Archangel Mariel or calling his name will draw his light to you and help you attune to his energy.
- Ask Archangel Mariel to help you bring forward your soul gifts and talents.
- Ask Archangel Mariel to enfold you in his immense wings and help you merge your earthly and divine wisdom.
- Ask Archangel Lavender to connect you to the wisdom of the divine feminine.
- Ask Archangel Lavender to enfold you with her gentle lavender light to access your ancient wisdom and bring you healing while you sleep.
- You can ask Archangel Lavender to communicate with people on your behalf to resolve forgiveness issues.

- Say the affirmation "I AM Archangel Mariel."
  I AM affirmations are powerful because they draw to you what
  you are affirming. If you say, "I AM Archangel Mariel," your
  highest-dimensional aspect merges with Archangel Mariel,
  and you draw his amazing qualities to you.
- Visit Archangels Mariel and Lavender at their spiritual retreat
  when you sleep at night in order to access their teachings.

Meet Ascended Master Lord Kuthumi

Lord Kuthumi holds the title of World Teacher and helps people
learn and understand spiritual concepts. He is famous for bringing
theosophy to the world and inspiring Madame Blavatsky with her
writings about the ascended masters. He belongs to the Brotherhood
of the Golden Robe, who take on the pain of the world. In his past
incarnations, he lived as Melchior, one of the three wise men who
visited Jesus, and he was Pythagoras who introduced sacred geometry,
numerology, mathematics, and the music of the spheres. He incarnated as Shah Jahan, who built the Taj Mahal out of love for his wife,
and St Francis of Assisi, who was known for his love of animals. He
has a spiritual retreat above Kashmir in Agra, India, and an ascension
chamber above Machu Picchu, Peru.

Tips on How to Interact with Ascended Master Lord Kuthumi

- You can ask Lord Kuthumi to help you with learning
  and understanding spiritual truths.
- You can visit his ascension chamber above Machu Picchu
  when you sleep at night and receive his teachings to accelerate
  your ascension path.
- You can say the affirmation "I AM Lord Kuthumi"
  to increase the light you carry and to draw his qualities
  to you.
- You can imagine a six-pointed Star of David, Lord Kuthumi's
  symbol, and connect with his energy.

- You can ask Lord Kuthumi to help you return with love those energies that are not your own to the person they belong to.

VISUALIZATION to Accelerate Your Evolution and Embody Your Soul

1. Sit in your Gen area. Close your eyes and relax.
2. Call your angel of the home, your guardian angel, and your personal unicorn and dragon to come close.
3. Take yourself into the mountainous Gen area. You are standing at the foot of a mountain and see a winding path. Breathe in the fresh air, and feel a breeze caressing your face. As you look up into the sky, you can see a majestic bird soaring high.
4. Before starting to climb, take a moment to take your awareness to your Earth Star chakra below your feet. Visualize big, strong, silvery roots growing all the way down into the centre of the earth, grounding you deeply. Your unicorn whispers in your ear, "I am grounded into the loving heart of Mother Earth," and you mentally repeat these words.
5. Your dragon moves ahead of you and clears the path with its flames. See the path lighting up with platinum light. Your unicorn whispers, "I AM Love," and you repeat these words.
6. As you continue, the path becomes pink, and your unicorn whispers, "I feel love," and you repeat these words.
7. After a while, the path turns orange, and your unicorn whispers, "I create love," and you repeat this affirmation.
8. The path next turns golden, and your unicorn whispers, "I take action with love," and you repeat these words.
9. The path changes into pure white with tinges of pink, and your unicorn prompts you to say, "I love with all my heart."
10. As the path continues to climb, its white colour changes to blue, and as you look at your unicorn, it whispers, "I speak with love," and you repeat these words.

135

11. The blue of the path now turns crystal clear with an emerald glow, and your unicorn whispers, "I see with love," and you repeat these words.

12. The next colour change in the path is crystal clear with a golden glow. But before your unicorn can suggest the next words, you become aware of a mighty golden angel. "I AM Archangel Jophiel," he tells you. You bow to the angel in awe, and with a hand gesture, he encourages you to say these words in response: "I know love." He keeps gesturing, and you mentally repeat them while he holds his hand above your crown chakra. You can see golden light pouring from his hand into your crown chakra, energizing your knowledge. It flows down through your chakra column and energy fields, flooding you with cosmic wisdom. When the work is complete, Archangel Jophiel nods and indicates that you should continue on your path now.

13. The moon has risen, and the path below your feet is the same colour as the moonlight. Your dragon's flames and your unicorn's light are so bright you can see perfectly. You are reaching a bridge now. Below the bridge, there is a river that flows down the mountains and across the valleys. It is a long and far-reaching river, shimmering under the moonlight. The bridge is shining in bright rainbow colours, but you can see the colour magenta above all.

14. You cross the bridge with your dragon and unicorn in 11 steps. As you step onto the other side, the path is magenta. Once more, a mighty archangel with a glorious magenta aura meets you. His heart radiates pure love, and his wisdom is as far-reaching as the universe. You look at him in wonder and bow. This is the Archangel Mariel.

15. Archangel Mariel puts his hand on his heart and greets you with a melodic voice. You wonder why he has come to meet you. He takes you by the hand and silently walks the last bit of the magenta path with you to the top of the mountain. Above the

mountain, a golden mist glows. Through the mist, you can see the outline of a bigger mountain. Archangel Mariel tells you the last of the words, "I AM the soul," and while you repeat them, he touches the Soul Star chakra above your head, making it expand.

16. Archangel Mariel now takes you into his arms and flies up with you into the ether. You can see a golden temple now flooded in the light of the moon and the stars. The guardian of the temple bows and lets you enter.

17. You walk along a corridor with Archangel Mariel, your dragon, and your unicorn. Archangel Mariel takes you into a teaching hall where Lord Kuthumi conducts his teachings. You have the opportunity to listen to the great ascended master. Many disciples sit here, and Archangel Mariel suggests you take a seat.

18. Even if you cannot hear the words, tune into the energy. Lord Kuthumi is talking to his initiates about the Soul Merge. On the inner planes, this is considered the first major initiation. He is imparting techniques to his initiates to help humans achieve this initiation. Think, feel, speak, and act as though the soul is the essence of his message. Your soul is not something separate that you have to connect to; you are a walking soul here on Earth, and its vast consciousness is always available to you.

19. Lord Kuthumi has noticed your presence in his hall and smiles at you. You bow with awe. He approaches and takes you outside to the courtyard into a beautiful garden. Here, you have the opportunity to talk to Lord Kuthumi about the Soul Merge and what it means to you to be one with your soul. Take a few minutes for this.

20. Lord Kuthumi takes you to the temple exit, but before you leave, he invites you to visit his training establishment at night when you sleep. Here, you can learn to fully embody your soul to express its essence through your physical vehicle. Thank Lord Kuthumi for the invitation and all the insights received.

21. Archangel Mariel takes you back to the mountaintop.
    He points to the higher mountain behind, and you see a
    magnificent-coloured sphere of light hovering above it.
    Archangel Mariel explains that this is your Monad, your
    highest-dimensional aspect, and you will meet with it soon.
    Then he takes you into his arms and flies you swiftly down the
    mountain, followed by your dragon and unicorn.

22. You are back in your space now. Breathe deeply, and bring your
    awareness fully into your physical body.

CONNECT with the Number Eight

The number eight symbolizes balance and infinity. It inspires you with
powerful ambitions, visions, and big dreams and projects. When you
embody your soul on Earth, you have the confidence, courage, and
determination to make your dreams a reality. Number eight brings
you infinite possibilities, and in its highest expression, it transforms
the world.

1. Close your eyes, and take a deep breath.
2. Visualize the turtle rising from the clear river water and observe
   the map on its back. The area with eight dots is illuminated.
3. As you observe the glowing dots, the turtle transports you on its
   spacious back and lifts you to the ninth-dimensional pool of the
   number eight out in the universe.
4. The turtle lands in the pool, and the powerful energy flows into
   you, filling you with the divine qualities to embody your soul
   fully.
5. Absorb the energy of balance, powerful ambitions, big dreams,
   high-frequency visions, and projects, and the confidence,
   courage, and determination to complete them and make them
   a reality.
6. Send heartfelt gratitude to the turtle for inspiring you with
   infinite possibilities.

Intention for the Gen Area of Your Life

*"I fully embody my soul and express its essence through
my physical vehicle. I AM the soul."*

Please repeat this affirmation for the coming week, or write your own
for the Gen area.

LI – Your True Magnificence

BAGUA AREA 9

This area of your bagua is called Li. The energy of the Li area is yang/yin/yang, and it is associated with the middle daughter, a passionate and generous energy. Li symbolizes fire, and its element is earth. Li traditionally represents fame. On my 5D Bagua of Higher Aspirations, I have called it Your True Magnificence.

I have given this bagua area a golden colour like the Stellar Gateway chakra. In this centre, you access your highest-dimensional aspect, the Monad.

This area traditionally concerns your reputation, self-worth, and how people see you. But at a higher level, it is about knowing who you truly are and sacred integrity. Wise, evolved people have a certain aura, and they radiate so much light that people cannot help noticing them. Evolved people feel inspired and satisfied with their work, projects, and activities. Light is a keyword for this area. In this chapter, we will work to connect you with your Monad. The Monad, also known as the I AM Presence, is the original divine spark that Source created. It is your divine aspect, your divine self.

Monad Note

In the beginning, Source created divine sparks, which we can call Monad, I AM Presence, or Divine Self. The Monad is your connection with Source and your highest-dimensional aspect. To expand creation, the Monad sent forth 12 souls. This means you have 11 soul brothers and sisters who share the same Monad. To expand further, your soul sent forth 12 extensions, one of which is your personality here on

Earth. This makes up your Monadic family of 144. After the soul merge, your soul starts to reach up to your Monad, and your Monad sends its light down to your soul. When they merge you pass your fifth initiation, and your Monad becomes your teacher and its immense wisdom guides you forward on your ascension path.

Personal Note on My Li Area

My Li area falls onto my very bright bedroom with a large window. This is also where I have anchored a portal of light, where light beings can visit me and share their wisdom and light, facilitate spirit travel into the higher dimension, and link me with stars and high-frequency energies. I will add another intention to this portal: receive guidance from my highest-dimensional aspect.

I also want to activate the Li area in my living room. Here, it falls in front of the window, and the space is absolutely clear of anything. This means the energy can flow perfectly, and there is much light. And the high-frequency energy from the ascension column I have anchored into the centre of this room can flow into it. Now, have a look at where your Li area is, and let's clear it.

VISUALIZATION to Clear the Li Area

1. Sit in the space that represents the Li area in your home.
2. You may wish to light a candle and burn some incense.
3. Close your eyes and relax. Breathe deeply into your heart.
4. Set the intention to clear this area to facilitate access to your highest-dimensional aspect.
5. Call your angel of the home to supervise and hold the light. Call in your guardian angel and your personal unicorn and dragon to come close.
6. First, invoke a fire dragon. Maybe your personal dragon is a fire dragon; if so, it can clear the area with its blazing flames.
7. Next, invoke Ascended Master Serapis Bey, and ask him to flood this area with the ascension flame. Visualize yourself sitting,

and white flames are blazing through you and around you and through the whole area. Feel the shift in frequency.

8. Ask your unicorn to add its light.
9. Ask the angel of your home to fill this space with love.
10. Have a chat with all beings present and check whether you need to change anything here.
11. Thank them for the cleansing and insights.
12. Come back with your consciousness into your physical body, and open your eyes.

EXERCISE: Who Are You?

For this area, I would like you to do an exercise to deepen your understanding of who you truly are. The exercise permits you to think beyond the roles you hold and the activities you carry out. Your guardian angel will support and inspire you. You will need a pen and paper and to keep writing for 10 minutes so that you can go really deep, so please set a timer.

1. Imagine your guardian angel is seated in front of you and asks, "Who are you?" Start brainstorming, and write everything that comes into your mind.
2. Your guardian angel asks again, "Who are you?" This time, go deeper. Who are you, really? Come up with more.
3. Your guardian angel asks again, "Who are you?" Go even deeper. Who are you at the highest level, not only planetary but universal?
4. When the 10 minutes have passed, read what you have written. Reflect on whether you feel more aligned with your soul intentions and your true magnificence.

Your Evolution and the Monadic Merge

In the next visualization, you will once more journey up a mountain. This mountain represents your highest-dimensional aspect, the Monad, or I AM Presence. In this visualization, you will hear about the

Monadic Merge, which happens when completing the fifth initiation on the ascension path. In the previous chapter, we discussed the third initiation, the Soul Merge. The fourth initiation requires you to let go of any attachments and crucify your lower nature. You may be required to leave a job or work part-time so that you can start doing what you love, or you may have to leave a relationship that is holding you back. You may need to make room in your life to be truly yourself.

The fourth initiation attunes you to your Monad so that you can take guidance from it. This is probably a very exciting time for you and involves taking action. Service becomes a priority as you enter more and more into your mission, and abundance is an automatic consequence.

At the completion of the fifth initiation, you experience the Monadic Merge and embody the consciousness of your Monad here on Earth at a deeper level. You will make a big impact on people. Before doing the visualization, please read the information about Archangel Metatron.

Meet Archangel Metatron

Archangel Metatron is the mightiest of the mighty and radiates a glorious colour frequency from deep gold to orange and red. He is in charge of the ascension process and connects with people who are dedicated to the ascension path. As the creator of all light, he can help you to increase your light quotient. He is also known as the Heavenly Scribe, who transmits the orders of Source to all the archangels and is the only archangel allowed to look directly at the Creator. Archangel Metatron is in charge of developing the Stellar Gateway chakra of all of humanity at a fifth-dimensional level. His spiritual retreat is above Luxor, Egypt. His twin flame is Archangel Sandalphon.

Tips on How to Interact with Archangel Metatron

- Connect with Archangel Metatron by thinking or saying his name and visualizing his golden-orange ascension energy.

- You can ask Archangel Metatron to step into your aura and increase the light in all of your cells.
- Say the affirmation "I AM Archangel Metatron" to draw his powerful qualities to you.
- You can ask your spirit to visit Archangel Metatron's spiritual retreat above Luxor when you sleep to help you accelerate your ascension.
- Call upon Archangel Metatron to expand your Stellar Gateway chakra.

VISUALIZATION to Merge with Your Monad

1. Sit in your Li area. Close your eyes and relax.
2. Call your personal unicorn and dragon to come close.
3. Visualize yourself standing at the foot of a mountain. This is a higher and steeper mountain than the one you climbed before, and you see fire dragons flying around it.
4. There is a path leading up. Your unicorn nudges you and invites you to climb onto its back. You gladly accept and start the ascent. Your dragon is flying ahead, making sure the way is clear. The path is lined with blazing flames, and if you look carefully, you can see beautiful salamanders working to keep the flames alive. The salamanders are the guardians of fire.
5. The unicorn climbs the path easily, stepping over stones or flying over big rocks. As before, the path is changing colour. It starts off shining with a silvery light and then bright platinum. After a while, it becomes a delicate pink, then a bright orange.
6. As you ascend further, it turns bright gold. At this point, a mighty, deep-golden angel appears on the path in all his glory. "I am Archangel Uriel," he tells you. You look at him in awe and bow. His light creates a sense of peace in your heart and mind.

7. Archangel Uriel shows you a golden flame in the palm of his hand. With your permission, he puts it into your solar plexus. As this surge of energy enters your solar plexus, feel it warming up and expanding. It blazes like a fiery sun, and you receive a boost of self-worth and confidence in your unique skills to be used to help Earth shift into the new Golden Age. Thank Archangel Uriel for what you have received, and watch him leave.

8. The unicorn continues to climb higher and higher. The path is now pure white. After a while, it becomes electric blue and then crystal clear with an emerald glow.

9. As you climb even higher, the path remains crystal clear but is now glowing with gold. After a while, it becomes moon white and then turns magenta and blue. You are almost at the top of the mountain now, and the view is breathtaking. Your unicorn and dragon smile at you; they are very pleased that you have come this far.

10. You are standing in front of a bridge hanging over a void. It is sloping upwards, so the other side is higher than where you are standing. You look over the edge and gaze upon the deepest drop you have ever seen and a stream flowing over big rocks. It takes courage to cross this bridge, but it is perfectly possible with willpower and taking one step after another.

11. Both sides of the bridge start to blaze with extraordinary golden-orange flames. You wonder what kind of fire it is. Your dragon is an expert and tells you, "It's cosmic fire."

12. Suddenly, your guardian angel appears and tells you that you have to cross this bridge with your own feet. They gesture for you to dismount from your unicorn. You do as your angel says, and the angel takes your hand to offer support. Step onto the bridge. It moves a bit, but your angel is encouraging you to go forward. You cross it slowly, step by step. Take some time to do so.

Become aware that you are being cleansed at a deep level as you move between the cosmic fire.

13. When you reach the other side, you see the most magnificent angel you have ever seen. "I AM Archangel Metatron," he says. As soon as he has spoken these words, the golden-orange light around him increases and illuminates the whole area. He smiles kindly, and you bow.

14. The path that leads to the mountain summit also radiates golden-orange light. But before you continue your journey, Archangel Metatron raises his hand. Light flows from his fingers, and he directs it into your Stellar Gateway chakra, one meter above your head. He can easily do that as he towers high above you. The Stellar Gateway chakra holds the energy of your I AM Presence. The light flowing from Archangel Metatron's hands flows down your entire chakra column and fills all your energy fields, increasing the level of light you carry.

15. Archangel Metatron turns around and gestures for you to follow him. He leads you the last bit of the way to the mountaintop, and as you reach it, you can see the most glorious blazing sphere of light shining onto you like a sun. It is very close to you, and as you gaze at it with wonder, you feel your consciousness merging with it. You feel part of it and the immense wisdom and love it contains. The amount of light in and around you is amazing. You may become aware of your Monadic family, all the beings that make up your I AM Presence. You may also become aware of your light bodies activating and glowing with light, and you can use them to explore the universe. As you do so, you feel one with the whole of the universe, and all there is. You feel incredible expansion. Enjoy this for as long as you wish.

16. Very gently, bring your aura in a little bit, and return to the mountaintop. Archangel Metatron raises his hand once more to bless you and your path. Then he takes you into his arms and flies you swiftly down the mountain, followed by your

dragon and unicorn. Thank Archangel Metatron for all you have experienced, and see him retreat. Thank your dragon and unicorn.

17. Very slowly, bring your awareness back into your space, and bring the light from your Monad with you. Come fully into your physical body, and open your eyes.

CONNECT with the Number Nine

The number nine symbolizes completion, divine wisdom, enlightenment, and leadership. You are qualified to give service using your unique gifts. You are ready to give all and create for the higher good of humanity without looking for reward.

1. Close your eyes, and take a deep breath.
2. Visualize the turtle rising from the river and see nine glowing dots on its back.
3. The turtle smiles at you and transports you swiftly to the ninth-dimensional cosmic pool of number 9. You bathe and receive the keys and codes from the pool and the turtle.
4. The energy is streaming into you and lighting you up with the highest qualities of number nine: completion, divine wisdom, enlightenment, leadership, and creating for the highest good of humanity.
5. Send your gratitude to the turtle for the wisdom it brought you.

Intention for the Li Area of Your Life

"I am crossing the spiritual bridge that allows me to merge with my mighty I AM Presence. I AM the Monad. I AM love. I AM light. I AM power."

Please repeat this affirmation for the coming week, or write your own for the Li area.

Summary

Congratulations, you have reached almost the end of this book, and it is time to review your progress and experiences. I would like to invite you to walk through your home. Feel into the changed energy in each space, and reflect on whether it supports you and whether transformations have happened in your life. Please take your floor plan with the 5D Bagua of Higher Aspirations imposed upon it to orient yourself.

Bagua Area 1: KAN – Your Life Mission

Walk into the space (or spaces) where you have activated your Kan area. How does it feel? Has the energy changed? Do you feel the space supports your life mission? Has anything changed in your life regarding your purpose since you started this programme? Please take some time to journal and think about what your soul has decided to learn and achieve in this lifetime and then write your reflections.

Bagua Area 2: KUN – Your Beautiful Open Heart

Walk into the space where you have activated your KUN area. How does it feel? Do you feel that energy supports you in opening your heart, healing your relationships, and seeing with the eyes of love? Think about the relationships in your life. Have they improved since you started this work? Please reflect and take some time to journal.

Bagua Area 3: ZHEN – The Gifts of the Ancestors

Walk into the space where you have activated Zhen. How does it feel? Has the energy changed? Do you feel the positive energy of your ancestors supporting you? Do you feel your foundation for the work that you have come to do is stronger? Do you feel deeply grounded into the planet and loved by Mother Earth? Write down your reflections.

Bagua Area 4: XUN – Open up to Abundance

Walk into the areas where you have activated Xun. How does it feel? Has the energy changed? On a level of 1 – 10, where is your abundance consciousness right now? Does the energy here support you in accessing the infinite abundance of the Universe? Are you open to receiving and giving in a balanced way? Has anything changed since you started the programme? Write down your thoughts.

Bagua Area 5: TAIJI Centre – Balance and Glorious Health

Walk into the space where you have activated the Taiji centre, representing yourself and your divine essence. How does it feel? Has the energy changed? Does it support balance within you, glorious health, and a harmonious life? Do you feel energized and healthier? Jot down your reflections.

Bagua Area 6: QIAN – Incredible Higher Help

Walk into the space where you have activated Qian. How does the energy feel? Does it facilitate your connection with higher beings? Do you get a sense that you are never alone and very much supported at every moment in your life? Do you feel a closer connection with your guardian angel and all the beings that make up your ascension team? Write down your reflections.

Bagua Area 7: DUI – Never-Ending Creativity

Walk into the space where you have activated Dui. Has the energy changed? How do you feel? Does this space facilitate divine inspiration and exciting ideas to come to you? Do you feel bubbling with creativity and motivated to start projects and complete them? Jot down your thoughts.

Bagua Area 8: GEN – Embodying Your Soul

Walk into the Gen area. How do you feel here? Has anything changed since you started the programme? Does the energy here reflect the beauty and wisdom of your soul? Does it facilitate you embodying your soul, expressing your divine essence, and sharing your unique talents and gifts with the world? Reflect and write down your thoughts.

Bagua Area 9: LI – Your True Magnificence

Finally, walk into the space where you have activated Li. How does it feel? Has the energy changed? Does it facilitate you receiving guidance from your highest-dimensional aspect? How do you think people see you now? How do you see yourself? Have you understood how truly magnificent you are? Write down your reflections.

Now that you have reviewed your progress, it is probably clear whether some areas need more work, be it energetic or physical tidying and rearranging (see the next chapter). You can focus on and work through the relevant chapters again with your support team and repeat the exercises and visualizations as often as you feel necessary to align with your fifth-dimensional possibilities. Perfection is not required while incarnated in a human body, but remember, every day is an opportunity to grow and learn, and with your divine helpers, anything is possible.

Serious Decluttering

You have reached the final chapter, and I have something more to share with you. While working on finalizing this book, it just so happened that several people mentioned the Japanese author Marie Kondo, the queen of tidying up, to me. I realized that it was a nudge from the Universe to buy her book and watch some of her shows. I understood that my guides were literally pushing me to take decluttering to another level.

It takes a lot of courage and a leap of faith to follow through with what Marie Kondo teaches. The first step of her method is to throw all your clothes onto the bed or the ground, and she means every single item, including shoes and bags. You then touch and connect with each item of clothing and decide whether it sparks joy for you. If it does, you keep it; if it doesn't, you discard it with gratitude and give thanks for the purpose it had in your life. Only after you go through this process do you start putting your clothes back into the wardrobe and drawers, folded in a very special and caring way. You create a rectangle and fold it down until it stands.

I hadn't even finished reading Marie's book when, one day, I decided to get started with my son Ferrante's clothes. He is neuro-diverse and not able to sort out his clothes, so I asked my daughter Artemisia to help me. We threw all his clothes into a pile on the bed, touched each item together, and decided whether to keep or discard it. Interestingly, we were very much aligned with what sparked joy and what didn't and made quick progress. Ferrante was with us, watching with interest. I am sure he was pleased that we took care of his clothes in such a way. After we experimented with folding and storing them in this new way, we found that suddenly there was space for everything, and it looked so nice and tidy. I felt deeply satisfied and grateful for having discovered this technique, and I am sending blessings to Marie Kondo as I write this.

A few days later, I felt ready and courageous enough to sort through my own clothes. My schedule is always very busy, but I knew I had to do this, because I was meant to share my experience in this book.

This was a much bigger job. Once you remove the clothes from the wardrobe, there is no turning back, but I underestimated how long it would take to sort it out. I went through the process of choosing and discarding, but afterwards, I only managed to put half my clothes back into the wardrobe, so I had to sleep one night with half of my bed still full of clothes. I was grateful I managed to clear some space for sleeping and felt so good because I knew the rest could be easily sorted out the next day.

I felt immense happiness when I completed it. It was a great feeling to see the space cleared and have an overview of my clothes because, by storing them in this new way, you can see what you have at a glance, and that is both your winter and summer clothes because, with Marie Kondo's technique, you don't separate them.

Next, I helped Artemisia with her clothes. By the time we finished, we had about 20 bags in the corridor to be discarded. I held onto them for a while before I finally had the courage to take them to the appropriate clothes disposal place.

The rest of the house can be done in the same way. Marie advises that the next major item to sort through is books and then all other miscellaneous things. She says to sort by category, not by location and ensure every item has its place. That way, you will always know where to put something, and you will always find it. I can wholeheartedly recommend this approach.

Bibliography

Brown, Simon. *The Feng Shui Bible: The Definitive Guide to Improving Your Life, Home, Health, and Finances, Volume 4* (Mind Body Spirit Bibles). New York: Sterling/Union Square & Co., 2005.

Cooper, Diana. *The Golden Future: What to Expect and How to Reach the Fifth Dimension.* London: Hay House UK, 2023.

———. *The Magic of Unicorns: Help and Healing from the Heavenly Realms.* London: Hay House UK, 2020.

———. *Dragons: Your Celestial Guardians.* London: Hay House UK, 2018.

———. *Angel Inspiration: How to Change the World with Your Angels.* New York: Hachette/Mobius books, 2004.

———. *Transform Your Life: A Step-by-Step Programme for Change.* New York: Little Brown/Piatkus, 1998.

Cooper, Diana, and Kathy Crosswell. *Keys to the Universe: Access the Ancient Secrets by Attuning to the Wisdom and Power of the Cosmos.* Scotland: Findhorn Press, 2010.

Cooper, Diana, and Tim Whild. *Archangel Guide to Enlightenment and Mastery: Visualizations for Living in the Fifth Dimension.* CD. London: Hay House UK, 2016.

Kondo, Marie. *The Life-Changing Magic of Tidying: A Simple, Effective Way to Banish Clutter Forever.* London: Penguin Random House/Vermilion, 2014.

Exercises and Visualizations

PREPARATION WEEK

VISUALIZATION to Connect with the Angel of Your Home 30

EXERCISE to Programme a Crystal to Help You
Transform Your Home 33

EXERCISE to Ask a Network of Rose Quartz Crystals to
Stream Love into Your Home 33

VISUALIZATION to Clear the Energies below Your Home with an
Earth Dragon 35

VISUALIZATION to Clear the Energies around Your Home with
Angels and Dragons 36

INVOKE Your Home Transformation Team 38

DRAW Your Bagua 42

WEEK 1

VISUALIZATION to Clear the Kan Area with a Water Dragon 47

VISUALIZATION to Meet Your Personal Unicorn and Receive
Its Name 52

VISUALIZATION to Activate Your Life Mission with the
Diamond Unicorns 53

CONNECT with the Number One 57

WEEK 2

VISUALIZATION to Clear the Kun Area 61

VISUALIZATION to Meet Your Personal Dragon and
Receive Its Name 64

VISUALIZATION with Kuan Yin to Open Your Heart to
Divine Feminine Love and Forgiveness 66

CONNECT with the Number Two 69

WEEK 3

VISUALIZATION to Clear the Zhen Area 72

VISUALIZATION to Honour Your Immediate Ancestors 75

VISUALIZATION to Meet Your Parents in Their Spirit Body 78

VISUALIZATION to Meet Your Cosmic Parents 80

CONNECT with the Number Three 83

WEEK 4

VISUALIZATION to Clear the Xun Area 87

VISUALIZATION to Activate Your Abundance Codes 93

CONNECT with the Number Four 95

WEEK 5

VISUALIZATION to Clear the Taiji Centre and Activate it 99

VISUALIZATION to Activate Your Taiji Centre with a
Portal of Light 105

VISUALIZATION to Restore Balance and Glorious Health 109

CONNECT with the Number Five 112

WEEK 6

VISUALIZATION to Clear the Qian Area 115

VISUALIZATION to Receive Your Guardian Angel's Name 118

VISUALIZATION to Visit Your Overlighting Archangel 121

CONNECT with the Number Six 124

WEEK 7

VISUALIZATION to Clear the Dui Area 126

VISUALIZATION to Bring Forth Your Creativity 127

CONNECT with the Number Seven 129

WEEK 8

VISUALIZATION to Clear the Gen Area 131

VISUALIZATION to Accelerate Your Evolution and
Embody Your Soul 135

CONNECT with the Number Eight 138

WEEK 9

VISUALIZATION to Clear the Li Area 141

EXERCISE: Who Are You? 142

VISUALIZATION to Merge with Your Monad 144

CONNECT with the Number Nine 147

About the Author

Photo by Paulina Ierrubino

Franziska is an international author, ascension leader, and principal teacher of the Diana Cooper School of White Light, with the mission of raising consciousness and serving as a bridge between the heavens and Earth. She works with angels, unicorns, and dragons to help people accelerate their ascension. Aspiring spiritual teachers come to Franziska for certified training in how to share the wisdom of the angels, unicorns, and dragons in order for Earth to shift into the fifth dimension.

For more information, workshops, and events visit:

https://franziskasiragusa.com
https://www.youtube.com/@FranziskaSiragusa
www.facebook.com/FranziskaHigherAscension

Index

5D colour chart, 44
11D Energy of Regeneration, 107–11

A
abundance, 84, 89, 93–95
air dragon, 85–86
ancestors, 71–77
angels, 18–22
  angel of your home, 29–31
  guardian angel, 18–19, 116–19
archangels, 21, 120
  Archangel Amethyst, 104
  Archangel Aurora, 120–21
  Archangel Chamuel, 60–61
  Archangel Christine, 101–9
  Archangel Faith, 43
  Archangel Gabriel, 52–55
  Archangel Jophiel, 101–2
  Archangel Lavender, 133–34
  Archangel Mary, 102–3
  Archangel Metatron, 143–44
  Archangel Michael, 43
  Archangel Raphael, 86–88
  Archangel Sandalphon, 103–4
  Archangel Uriel, 120–21
  Archangel Zadkiel, 104
ascended masters
  Lord Kuthumi, 134–37
  Serapis Bey, 98–99
ascension column, 99

B
bagua, 39–42
base chakra, 91

C
chakras, 89–95
  12 chakra system, 89–93
  causal chakra, 92–93
  crown chakra, 92
  earth star chakra, 90
  heart chakra, 91–92
  navel chakra, 91
  sacral chakra, 91
  solar plexus chakra, 91
  Soul Star chakra, 93
  Stellar Gateway chakra, 93
  third-eye chakra, 92
  throat chakra, 92
cherubim, 21–22
Cooper, Diana, 13, 73, 89
Cosmic Diamond Violet Flame, 105
cosmic parents, 80–82
cosmic turtle, 56
creativity, 125, 127–29
crystals, 31–33

D
declutter, 37, 151–52
diamond unicorns, 49–50, 53–56
dominions, 21
dragons, 24–25
  air dragon, 85–86

earth dragon, 34–35
gold and silver violet flame dragon,
35-37
water dragon, 46–48
yin and yang dragons, 108, 111–2
Dui, bagua area 7, 125–29

E
earth dragon, 34–35
earth star chakra, 90

G
Gen, bagua area 8, 130–39
gold and silver violet flame dragon,
35-37
golden age, 17
guardian angel, 18–19, 116–19

H
health, 97, 106–7, 109–12
heart, 58, 66–69
  heart chakra, 91–92
home transformation team, 37–38

K
Kan, bagua area 1, 45–57
karma, 73–75
Kuan Yin, goddess, 65–69
Kun, bagua area 2, 58–70

L
Li, bagua area 9, 140–47
life mission, 46, 53–56
Lords of Karma, 73–74

M
Monad, 140–41
Monadic Merge, 142–46

N
navel chakra, 91

P
parents, 78–79
portal of light, 101, 105–6
powers, 21
principalities, 21

Q
Qian, bagua area 6, 114–24

R
rose quartz, 33

S
sacral chakra, 91
seraphim, 22
solar plexus chakra, 91
Soul Merge, 133–34
Soul Star chakra, 93
Stellar Gateway chakra, 93

T
Taiji centre, bagua area 5, 97–113
third-eye chakra, 92
throat chakra, 92
thrones, 21

U
unicorns, 23–24, 48–52

V
virtues, 21

W
water dragon, 46–48

X
Xun, bagua area 4, 84–96

Y
yin and yang dragons, 108, 111–2

Z
Zhen, bagua area 3, 71–83

FINDHORN PRESS

Life-Changing Books

Learn more about us and our books at
www.findhornpress.com

For information on the Findhorn Foundation:

www.findhorn.org